BEYOND MCDONAL ＿Ａ ＩＩＵＮ

Beyond McDonaldization provides new concepts of higher education for the twenty-first century in a unique manner, challenging much that is written in mainstream texts. This book undertakes a reassessment of the growth of McDonaldization in higher education by exploring how the application of Ritzer's four features *efficiency, predictability, calculability* and *control* has become commonplace.

This wide-ranging text discusses arguments surrounding the industrialisation of higher education, with case studies and contributions from a wide range of international authors. Written in an accessible style, *Beyond McDonaldization* examines questions such as:

- Can we regain academic freedom whilst challenging the McDonaldization of thought and ideas?
- Is a McDonaldization of every aspect of academic life inevitable?
- Will the new focus on student experience damage young people?
- Why is a McDonaldized education living on borrowed time?
- Is it possible to recreate the university of the past or must we start anew?
- Does this industrialisation meet the educational needs of developing economies?

This book brings international discussions on the changing world of higher education and the theory of McDonaldization together, seeking to provide a positive future vision of higher education. Analysing and situating the discussion of higher education within a wider social, political and cultural context, this ground-breaking text will have a popular appeal with students, academics and educationalists.

Dennis Hayes is Professor of Education at the University of Derby and the director of the campaign group Academics for Academic Freedom (AFAF).

BEYOND MCDONALDIZATION

Visions of Higher Education

Edited by Dennis Hayes

Routledge
Taylor & Francis Group

LONDON AND NEW YORK

First published 2017
by Routledge
2 Park Square, Milton Park, Abingdon, Oxon OX14 4RN

and by Routledge
711 Third Avenue, New York, NY 10017

Routledge is an imprint of the Taylor & Francis Group, an informa business

British Library Cataloguing in Publication Data
A catalogue record for this book is available from the British Library

Library of Congress Cataloging in Publication Data
Names: Hayes, Dennis, 1950- editor.
Title: Beyond McDonaldization : visions of higher education / edited by Dennis Hayes.
Description: Abingdon, Oxon ; New York, NY : Routledge, 2017. | Includes bibliographical references.
Identifiers: LCCN 2016044693 | ISBN 9781138282582 (hbk : alk. paper) | ISBN 9781138282599 (pbk : alk. paper) | ISBN 9781315270654 (ebk)
Subjects: LCSH: Education, Higher--Economic aspects. | Education, Higher--Aims and objectives. | Universities and colleges--Sociological aspects.
Classification: LCC LC67.6 .B49 2017 | DDC 378--dc23
LC record available at https://lccn.loc.gov/2016044693

ISBN: 978-1-138-28258-2 (hbk)
ISBN: 978-1-138-28259-9 (pbk)
ISBN: 978-1-315-27065-4 (ebk)

Typeset in Bembo
by Taylor & Francis Books

CONTENTS

ILLUSTRATIONS

Figures

Tables

CONTRIBUTORS

Phil Baty is editor at large of *Times Higher Education* magazine and editor of the *Times Higher Education World University Rankings*. He was named among the top 15 'most influential in education' by *The Australian* newspaper in 2012. Phil's publications include chapters for *Blue Skies: New Thinking about the Future of Higher Education* and for *Rankings and Accountability in Higher Education* (Unesco).

Dennis Hayes is Professor of Education at the University of Derby. He was the first (joint) President of the University and College Union, the largest post-compulsory union in the world and is the founder of the campaign group Academics for Academic Freedom (AFAF). Dennis was a member of the editorial board of the *Times Higher Education* magazine until 2016 and is the author and editor of many books, including *The Dangerous Rise of Therapeutic Education* (with Kathryn Ecclestone) and *It's Teaching Not Therapy*.

Clare Hornsby is the Founding Trustee and Director of Benedictus, the first Catholic liberal arts college in the United Kingdom. Benedictus offers foundation and honours programmes studying the traditional liberal arts in the Catholic intellectual tradition, combined with history, languages, arts and culture of Europe. Her publications include *Digging and Dealing in Eighteenth Century Rome* (with Ilaria Bignamini) and *The Impact of Italy: The Grand Tour and Beyond*.

Angus Kennedy is the convenor of the Institute of Ideas' educational initiative The Academy, which he established in 2011 as a modest attempt to demonstrate – over four days of reading and discussion – what university should be like and so rarely is. He is interested in and writes on the philosophy of freedom and is the author of *Being Cultured: In Defence of Discrimination*.

Adam Kissel is the Senior Program Officer, University Investments, at Charles Koch Foundation. He was previously a vice president at The Foundation for Individual Rights in Education (thefire.org), a nonpartisan rights organisation in Philadelphia. While at FIRE, he spoke about individual rights on college campuses across the United States. He continues to campaign and, in 2015, he organised a Free Speech England tour. He was the recipient of a First Prize in Education Reporting from the National Education Writers Association (2009) and is the author, with Sharon Browne, of the *Faculty Rights Handbook*.

Ruth Mieschbuehler is an education researcher and a lecturer in education studies at the University of Derby. She has a long-standing interest in understanding social inequalities, particularly in relation to higher education. Her PhD thesis, *The Minoritisation of Higher Education Students,* was a study of philosophical and pedagogical approaches to student educational experiences. A book based on her thesis will be published in 2016.

Sebastian Morello began his studies in the theatrical arts before turning his attention to philosophy, scripture, and theology. He studied first with the Community of St John before going on to further philosophy and theology studies in Rome with the Istituto del Verbo Incarnato. Sebastian studied at the Open University and is a lecturer and trainer at the Centre for Catholic Formation in London. He is also a faculty member of the Roman Forum as well as of the Benedictus Summer School programme.

James Panton is Head of Politics at Magdalen College School, Oxford, and an Associate Lecturer in Philosophy and Politics with the Open University. Previously he was a lecturer in Political Theory and Intellectual History at St John's College, Hertford College, and Balliol College, Oxford. James was a founding member of the pressure group The Manifesto Club, which campaigns against the hyper-regulation of everyday life. He is the co-editor of *Science versus Superstition: The Case for a New Scientific Enlightenment*. His 'Reflections of an Early Career Don' appeared in the second edition of *The Oxford Tutorial*.

Gavin Poynter is Professor Emeritus at the School of Social Sciences, University of East London. Among his many publications are *Restructuring in the Service Industries, Olympic Cities: 2012* and *The Remaking of London and London after Recession: A Fictitious Capital?*

George Ritzer is Distinguished University Professor of Sociology at the University of Maryland. He has served as Chair of the American Sociological Association's Sections on Theoretical Sociology and Organizations and Occupations. He won the ASA's Distinguished Contributions to Teaching Award in 2000. His seminal book, *The McDonaldization of Society* (1993), has been described as one of the most noteworthy sociology books of all time, with more than 100,000 copies in print and a dozen translations. Among his many other books are *The McDonaldization Thesis* (1998), *Enchanting a Disenchanted World* (1999) and *The McDonaldization Reader* (2002).

Austin Williams is associate professor at Xi'an Jiaotong-Liverpool University (XJTLU) in Suzhou, China, and founder of ChinaCommentary.org, a research centre that seeks to understand contemporary China. He is also the managing editor of www.MasterplanningtheFuture.org, the first independent, online architecture magazine in China, and author of *The Enemies of Progress: The Dangers of Sustainability* (2008).

FOREWORD: BEYOND THE CHEAP DEGREE FRANCHISE

The startling parallels between the franchised degree – one of the most popular forms of international education – and the franchised hamburger have been perfectly illustrated by Philip Altbach.

Altbach, founding director of the Centre for International Higher Education at Boston College, observed in a column in *Times Higher Education* magazine: 'McDonald's sells the right to brand its products as long as franchisees adhere to strict standards and policies: thus a Big Mac tastes the same in Chicago or Shanghai. "Inputs" (potatoes, meat, the "special sauce") are carefully monitored. Business practices are stipulated and the brand image closely monitored, although there is modest latitude for local adaptation – a Big Mac in Riyadh is halal, and one can find a "McPork" in Bucharest.'[1]

Pretty much exactly the same model applies to franchised degrees, with universities selling the right for international third-party partners to deliver their branded degrees, with similar controls on standards and polices, and with consistency over course ingredients, with room for the odd local tweak. But there is one significant difference, Altbach pointed out: 'a fast food franchise requires more thought and greater commitment than a degree franchise. The burger franchise, at least, requires investment in facilities and equipment, while education franchises simply need to rent space, with little additional investment from either side.'

International education is an extraordinarily positive force: it helps meet the exploding demand for a university education around the world, bring skills and opportunities to millions and drive forward emerging economies; it transforms individuals' life chances; it helps develop the global citizens that global societies need; it fosters intercultural understanding; and it helps foster new knowledge and new ways to understand the world.

But as well as being an inherent global good, international education is also big business.

A UK Government research paper from November 2014 took an audit of so-called 'trans-national education' in the UK – that is, higher education provision, including franchised degrees, where the degree is studied for and awarded outside the home country of the degree-awarding body. Their report, *The Value of Transnational Education to the UK*,[2] estimated a total UK transnational education revenue of almost £496 million for 2012/13.

According to the OECD, there are more than 416,000 international students studying inside the UK (second only to the US, with 784,000). The Universities UK International Unit reported in 2016 that non-UK students generate an estimated £11 billion for the UK economy.

And with commercial imperatives have predictably come compromises, and inevitably, scandals.

To take just the UK, amid cases reported by *Times Higher Education* magazine was a 1996 case where an institution was exposed for applying weak controls over the degrees it franchised to a Greek partner who paid in cash – brought back to Britain, auditors found to their horror, in brown envelopes. In early 1997 the National Audit Office revealed the existence of an 'unknown stock' of blank degree certificates held in Malaysia by another institution's agent.

Lord Dearing's 1997 *National Committee of Inquiry into Higher Education* felt compelled to raise the alarm about franchised degrees. Dearing warned that some overseas programmes were blighted by 'variability in the application of quality assurance policies', and it reported 'an occasional willingness for UK institutions to accept a learning environment which would not be considered suitable in the UK'. Franchising 'must not prejudice the assurance of quality and maintenance of standards', it said.

And while it is clear that such cases represent just a small minority of activity, it seems some have simply failed to heed the warnings. As was pointed out in *Times Higher Education* in January 2012, the UK Quality Assurance Agency has issued five 'limited confidence' judgements against universities over their control of overseas collaborations since it was founded, after Dearing, in 1997.

Indeed, a massive scandal over the University of Wales' activities in 'validating' a large number of degree courses provided overseas helped bring down the 118-year institution altogether, which no longer exists in its own right.

Quality control failures by the university in its overseas operations dated back to the mid-1990s, but incredible success in making money by expanding such activities without sufficient scrutiny proved fatal. An analysis of the university's accounts by *Times Higher Education* found that in 2002–03 the university was generating around £3 million a year, nearly 40 per cent of its income, by validating the degrees awarded by 55 different organisations overseas and 20 more inside the UK. By 2009–10 it had around 140 collaborative centres in 30 countries, generating more than £10 million a year.

It took the media – notably the BBC – to uncover a string of serious problems. In June 2011 a special review by the QAA under its 'concerns' procedure said that the university had been 'culpably credulous' in some of its due diligence.

For Roger Brown, professor of higher education at Liverpool Hope University, there was one clear culprit: financial pressure. And it is a pressure than can only increase. He told *Times Higher Education* that under current government policies, 'commercial and competitive pressures are going to increase'. Universities desperately keen to diversify their incomes are likely to further step up overseas activities, and the pressure to cut corners will not go away.

The UK is not alone here. International student mobility has exploded and is predicted to reach 7 million by 2020. As the world moves quickly from an elite higher education system to a mass system, with huge expansion of student numbers (150 million) and massive capacity challenges in developing countries with exploding middle classes, something of an international education free-for-all has emerged. And it is a free-for-all that many fear has crowded out the fundamental principal of higher education as a public good.

The concerns were powerfully and memorably expressed by Adam Habib, deputy vice-chancellor of research, innovation and advancement at the University of Johannesburg. He told the WorldViews conference on media and higher education in Toronto, organised by the Ontario Confederation of University Faculty Associations and others, in June 2011 that powerful western universities were manipulating 'the desperation of people whose university systems [have been] completely demolished' to make a 'fortune' from overseas branch campuses.

He told the audience that while hosting a visit of US universities to South Africa, 'I was struck by how many really manipulate the desperation of people whose university systems are completely demolished and utilise that opportunity to make a fortune so that they can pad the balance sheets,' he said.

Professor Habib said, *Times Higher Education* reported, that this was a problem that afflicted all unequal relationships across and inside continents. He pinned the blame on the move away from state support for higher education around the world: 'It is a problem that is increasing the more [universities] behave as private institutions, the more the state withdraws, the more we move towards a deregulated environment.'

The system, he said, 'demands that they run the balance sheets at a profit' and this 'forces them to behave in ways that fundamentally violate the social value [of a university]. We can simply say that universities have no social value, the job is to make money, the job is to run as for-profit institutions, so don't judge us as any different to anyone else. That is a legitimate point of view … But don't claim credibility for the social goals on the one hand and then behave in the most aggressive neoliberal manner on the other hand.'

A year later the rhetoric was stepped up by the secretary general of the Association of African Universities, who claimed there was a new 'slave trade' developing in global higher education. Olugbemiro Jegede, the founding vice-chancellor of the National Open University of Nigeria, told delegates attending the Association of International Education Administrators' conference in Washington DC in February 2012 that universities in wealthy nations intent on ramping up commercial international activities must not 'exploit inadequacies' in developing countries.

'Internationalisation is not about conquest … It is not about flouting national rules and regulations – because we know many universities outside of Africa who just walk into Africa and start flouting rules and regulations. This has always been the case. Africa has only supplied raw materials. First was the slave trade … Now we are being called upon to supply the brains to other parts of the world, and this is what I call 'the slave trade in education … We must redefine internationalisation … We must promote true universalisation of knowledge … We need to discourage financial exploitation of students and protect the vulnerable.'

So alarmed was it by the situation, the International Association of Universities (IAU) has been seeking to change the direction of travel. Its concerns were raised in a formal 'statement on internationalization: towards a century of cooperation: internationalization of higher education', adopted in 2000: 'The external brain drain and other negative consequences of poorly designed cooperative activities have at times even exacerbated the conditions in developing nations. In more recent times, commercial and financial interests have gained prominence in the internationalization process and threaten to displace the less utilitarian and equally valuable aspects of this enriching necessary transformation of higher education.'

In April 2012 the IAU published its important 'call for action', *Affirming Academic Values in Internationalization of Higher Education*.[3] The call 'requires all institutions to revisit and affirm internationalisation's underlying values, principles and goals, including but not limited to: intercultural learning; inter-institutional cooperation; mutual benefit; solidarity; mutual respect; and fair partnership … internationalization … requires institutions everywhere to act as responsible global citizens, committed to help shape a global system of higher education that values academic integrity, quality, equitable access and reciprocity.'

As demand for higher education continues to explode from the ever-growing ranks of the middle classes, and as states struggle to meet demand and embrace the private, often for-profit sector as a way to meet demand, it will be increasingly tough for the sector to rally firmly behind these laudable ideals.

Phil Baty, Editor-at-Large, *Times Higher Education*, and Editor, *Times Higher Education World University Rankings*

Notes

1 A version of Altbach's article, Franchising – the McDonaldization of higher education, is available here: https://ejournals.bc.edu/ojs/index.php/ihe/article/viewFile/8582/7714 (accessed 8 July 2016).
2 The BIS research paper is available on the government web site: https://www.gov.uk/government/uploads/system/uploads/attachment_data/file/387910/bis-14-1202-the-value-of-transnational-education-to-the-uk.pdf (accessed 8 July 2016).
3 The IAU call for action is available on their web site: http://www.iau-aiu.net/content/affirming-academic-values-internationalization-higher-education-call-action (accessed 8 July 2016).

1

BEYOND THE MCDONALDIZATION OF HIGHER EDUCATION

Dennis Hayes

McDonald's are good at McDonaldization. Universities are not good at McDonaldization. They do it badly, like many of the cheap faux-McDonald's burger outlets on high streets and side streets around the world. When you buy a McDonald's meal in any of their outlets around the world, it is nutritious (see Johnson 2013) and much the same everywhere – with slight local variations and bits on the side, such as beer in France, and you love it, or you don't.

Two years ago while researching for a paper which would revisit some of the themes of *The McDonaldization of Higher Education* (Hayes and Wynyard 2002), I was generally optimistic about the potential for challenging McDonaldizing tendenciesin universities (see Hayes and Wynyard 2016[1]). I was playful about what I called the 'McDonaldization Game' (see below). But, as the paper was going to press I became subject to the Weberian pessimism that afflicts George Ritzer, who coined the term 'McDonaldization' to describe industrial process of rationalisation that were expanding beyond industry into the cultural and educational spheres. The reason was a renewed awareness of the consequences of McDonaldization in higher education at individual, institutional and governmental levels. At the individual level I had an experience of how distressing and destructive the process can be. It concerns Academic Workload Planning (AWP). This is a system in use in many UK universities to allocate staff hours. Using a maximum number of hours – 1600 per annum – time is allocated for teaching to a maximum of 550 hours (a contractual requirement) and the rest for marking and administrative duties according to a variety of judgments or formulae. In many universities a variety of tariffs cover 'research and scholarship'. In the case I am about to discuss an allocation of 200 hours had been made in line with the standard tariff at my university.

A colleague came to see me in some distress because of what her line manager had said about an invitation she had been given to speak at a major conference.

The manager's response was that as she had used up her 200 hours for scholarly activity she would have to take annual leave if she wished to give her talk! Ridiculous and punitive bean counting of this sort is a result of applying assembly-line approaches to university life. But it seems academics are comfortable with this aspect of McDonaldization and don't see it as irrational. They may believe what their managers and their unions tell them, that AWP produces a better 'work–life balance'. There was nothing 'balanced' in this approach as far as my colleague was concerned. She experienced considerable disenchantment due to one of the 'irrationalities of rationality' (Ritzer 2002: 19).

At the institutional level I became more aware of how destructive the McDonaldization process is after reading Eric Margolis' personal account of his experience of McDonaldization at Arizona State University (ASU) from its rebranding in 2002 as 'The New American University' (Margolis 2013). It is a depressing picture. Margolis sees rebranding as the most visible aspect of McDonaldization. In order to meet the demands of the twenty-first century, ASU created 'transdisciplinary schools' so that the College of Liberal Arts and Sciences was composed of:

- Earth and Space Exploration
- Geographical Sciences and Urban Planning
- Historical, Philosophical and Religious Studies
- Human Communication
- Human Evolution and Social Change
- International Letters and Cultures Life Sciences
- Mathematical and Statistical Sciences
- Politics and Global Studies
- Social and Family Dynamics
- Social Transformation
- Transborder Studies

(Margolis 2013: 255)

As Margolis says, 'This is not simply about name changing, which might simply be amusingly pretentious. It is about disrupting the power of academic departments and their connections to larger disciplines and professional organizations. While there are sociologists in Communication, Justice and Social Inquiry, and so on, there is no department of sociology' (Margolis 2013: 255). In the UK in my own discipline of education similar name changes are common, with departments and centres being rebranded with new names such as 'Children, Families and Communities' and the ubiquitous label 'Wellbeing' as in 'Education, Health and Wellbeing'. The effect, if not the intention, is also to disrupt academic subjects and departments.

Furthermore, the whole university was subject to 'eight design aspirations' to 'guide ASU's transformation':

1. Leverage Our Place ASU embraces its cultural, socioeconomic and, physical setting.

2.   Transform Society ASU catalyzes social change by being connected to social needs.
3.   Value Entrepreneurship ASU uses its knowledge and encourages innovation.
4.   Conduct Use-Inspired Research ASU research has purpose and impact.
5.   Enable Student Success ASU is committed to the success of each unique student.
6.   Fuse Intellectual Disciplines ASU creates knowledge by transcending academic disciplines.
7.   Be Socially Embedded ASU connects with communities through mutually beneficial partnerships.
8.   Engage Globally ASU engages with people and issues locally, nationally and internationally.

(Margolis 2013: 257)

These statements are familiar from the mission statements of many UK universities, but Margolis underplays their potential damage to the disciplines. They are, he says 'either free-floating signifiers empty of content, or simply a publicist's restatement of what every university strives for' (Margolis 2013: 257). In reality, they direct the university towards extrinsic ends and away from the pursuit of knowledge for its own sake, something which is true of every mission statement.

Rebranding is something that is almost a constant in UK universities. Until I read Margolis I had thought such name changing to be 'amusingly pretentious' or politically opportunistic. The realisation that they constitute an attack on academic disciplines was new to me, and it was depressing.

Most depressing of all was the announcement at the governmental level of a further and even more destructive development in the ongoing process of McDonaldization. After reporting on the growth in national and international league tables for many years and thinking it couldn't get any worse, it did. The UK government announced it was going to introduce a Teaching Excellence Framework (TEF). What this means is slowly becoming clear, but even in setting out its ideas about the TEF, the House of Commons Business, Innovation and Skills Committee recognise that 86 per cent of students are satisfied with their course. Nevertheless, they aim 'to encourage excellent teaching for all students' (House of Commons Business, Innovation and Skills Committee 2016: 5). Writing in 2002 on the 'sophistry' of teacher training for higher education it was clear that teaching in universities was fine and university lecturers did not need teacher training courses or a professional body supporting teaching (see Hayes 2002). The same is true today, but we are about to have an exercise imposed upon the sector that will rival the Research Excellence Framework in its time-consuming and stultifying effects. The sector loves league tables, and vice-chancellors, National Teaching Fellows and university learning enhancement teams mostly welcome the TEF.

Universities in the UK and, to a lesser extent, in America are now McDonaldized, even if we do not see the golden arches over campus buildings (see Hayes and Ritzer, Chapter 3 in this volume, and Margolis 2013: 258). We may as well have them there because the McDonaldization of higher education has been unchallenged. Part of the reason for this is that the McDonaldization process is not a bureaucratic attempt to turn the university into a factory but to rationalise and improve higher education for students and academics. To understand why the process of McDonaldization fails in its original intention, we have to understand the process and its appeal. A good place to start is with the global appeal of McDonald's.

McDonald's: founding a university near you?

McDonald's has over 34,000 outlets worldwide and over 2,000 in China. It is hard not to be impressed by the growth and impact of McDonald's since Ray Kroc opened the first of his restaurants in Des Plaines, Illinois, on 15 April 1955. It was in Shanghai that McDonald's opened its eighth Hamburger University in 2010. The Hamburger University has also come a long way since Fred Turner, who was Ray Kroc's first grill man and subsequently senior chairman of McDonald's, founded the first in the basement of a McDonald's in Elk Grove Village, Illinois. Famously, McDonald's set up a $40 million Hamburger University in 1981 at its headquarters in Oak Brook, Illinois, and then six others worldwide. Shanghai Hamburger U. was set up at a cost of $250 million, but there is no training in hamburgerology on campus. The focus is on business management and efficiency and, with its 1 per cent student acceptance rate, it's harder to get into than Harvard. McDonald's expansion is a global success story, and there are positive reviews of its training and business programmes (Telegraph 2010; Epstein 2012; *Economist* 2013; Bloomberg News 2011; Chalabi and Burn-Murdoch 2013; McDonalds.com 2014).

In terms of cultural study, from its origins to the twenty-first century, McDonald's has seemingly landscaped an entirely new world culture. Through its expansion it has established food as a new social and political power broker with consequent communication norms and mores in an increasingly globalized world. It has created its own sign community by a variety of means with its own vocabulary and grammar. By changing our established conventions to food it has enabled a mutual reframing of us to our social context.

George Ritzer: the living embodiment of a concept

A similar sociological success story attaches to George Ritzer, who is recognized as the person who coined the term 'McDonaldization' in the 1980s (Ritzer 1983) and through numerous publications spread the concept around the world. Ritzer has cooked up a sociological industry and a popular way of looking at culture. His seminal work *The McDonaldization of Society* was first published in 1993 and is, at the time of writing, in its eighth edition. Translated into over a dozen languages and with sales in the hundreds of thousands of copies, it has been supplemented by other works, including CDs, and by other writers, including ourselves. Ritzer's success with the term comes in part from the fact that, as Krishan Kumar points out, it 'nicely points to the exemplary role of one of the most successful contemporary practitioners of Weberian rationalization' (Kumar 1995: 189). As the blurb on one edition says, it is popular with students because the book 'connects the everyday world of the "twenty-something" consumer with sociological analysis' (Fifth Edition, Ritzer 2008).

Reading *The McDonaldization of Society* it is easy to get carried away, as many students are, by its grandiose narrative and its sweeping claims: 'The contention of this text, however, is that McDonaldization and its "modern" characteristics are not only with us for the foreseeable future, but also are spreading their influence at an accelerating rate throughout the rest of society ... McDonald's will remain powerful until the nature of society has changed so dramatically that McDonald's is no longer able to adapt to it' (Ritzer 1993: 152, 159). That unspecified abstract 'change' is unlikely. Even Ritzer's newly coined rival, the 'Starbuckization of Society', though it suggests a powerful, softened McDonaldization with an emphasis on escape, education and quality, is emphatically rejected as a possible alternative explanatory metaphor 'with a clear and resounding – No!' (Ritzer 2008: 224).

McDonaldization is the global force which is affecting all of society in a way not previously explained in the narratives of Post-Fordism and bureaucratization. Consistent with those previous explanations of social change, Ritzer cautions that McDonaldization has negative and dehumanizing or 'irrational' consequences.

In order to explain his thesis, Ritzer sends out four horsemen of his particular apocalypse. As he says, 'many of us, either as individuals or as representatives of various institutions, have come to value efficiency, calculability, predictability, and control, and seek them out whether or not there are economic gains involved' (1993: 149). These four dimensions of McDonaldization can be forced into fitting almost any societal occurrence, so we can have McDoctors, McDentists, McChurch, McSex, McFamily and so the list goes on (for more examples, see *McDonaldization: The Reader* [Ritzer 2002, 2009]).

Part of the problem with the McDonaldization thesis is that it rests on shaky theoretical suppositions. This is largely drawn from the work of the German sociologist Max Weber, in particular the 'iron cage' metaphor in the *Protestant Ethic and the Spirit of Capitalism* (Weber 1930). This Ritzer utilizes in conjunction with Weber's ideas regarding the growth of bureaucracy in the West with its attendant rationalization process: 'McDonaldization is an amplification and extension of Weber's theory of rationalization' (Ritzer 2000: 23). Ritzer also takes from Weber's work what he perceives as general pessimism as to the way society is evolving.

Weber generally argued that technology, like everything else in culture, would be subsumed under a growing *cloak* of rationality. In a pessimistic turn about the perils of advancing technology and the growth of acquisitive greed it brought in its train, Ritzer assumes that Weber argued that the process was irreversible when he said, 'care for external goods should only lie on the shoulders of the saint like a light cloak which can be thrown aside at any moment. But fate decreed that the cloak should become an iron cage' (Weber 1930: 117).

The whole basis of Ritzer's McDonaldization thesis stems from this particular reading of Weber. It is, as Robin Wynyard and I have argued previously, based on treating Weber's important explanatory concepts in a somewhat cavalier way (Hayes and Wynyard 2002: 2–7). Rationalization gets short shrift, being simply replaced by the 'more timely' label 'McDonaldization' (Ritzer 1993: xiii), and Ritzer attempts to link other concepts into some explanatory format: rationality ⇒ bureaucracy ⇒ irrationality ⇒ iron cage. The difference is the cannibalisation of these ideas. The rationalisation process for Ritzer causes a world-wide materialistic 'iron cage' which is inevitable and inescapable. Weber saw that the 'iron cage' is the expression of the 'inexorable power' of material possessions over people (Weber 1930: 181) but allowed for the possibility of the cage door being opened in the future by some human agency, or 'prophets' as he calls them (Weber 1930: 182). Though both Weber and Ritzer share a similar pessimistic platform, '[f]or Weber, the cage door is at least slightly ajar, where for Ritzer it is firmly shut' (Hayes and Wynyard 2002: 7).

To return to the appeal of Ritzer's McDonaldization thesis to students, there is an ever present irony in the sociological foundation of his work. Ritzer has simply and cleverly McDonaldized Weber's thinking and reduced it to four easily digestible nuggets of thought: efficiency, predictability, calculability and control.

McDonaldization of higher education

In the first edition of *The McDonaldization of Society*, Ritzer paints a depressing picture of the university:

> The modern university has, in various ways, become a highly irrational place. Many students (and faculty members) are put off by the huge factory-like atmosphere in these universities. They might feel like automatons processed by the bureaucracy and the computer or even cattle being run through a meat processing plant. In other words, education in such settings can be a dehumanising experience.
>
> *(Ritzer 1993: 142)*

He also sees the student as a consumer, or customer, all too ready to complain: 'The impact of McDonaldization is clear, for example, in the way that students increasingly relate to professors as if they were workers in the fast-food industry. If the "service" in class is not up to their standards, students feel free to complain and even behave abusively towards their professors' (Ritzer 2008: 158).

This is a seductive picture of the contemporary university, and Ritzer's four criteria of McDonaldization seem to fit it well. In order to show why it enchants, I use the order of Ritzer's early paper (1983), which is also the one he uses when discussing Starbucks (2008: 224–225).

Efficiency

'Efficiency' in higher education means getting more and more students through the system, the process often disparagingly called 'massification'. In Britain the New

Labour government (1997–2010) aimed at getting 50 per cent of young people into university. Other ways of making the output of universities more efficient are the removal of formal examinations in favour of more varied modes of assessment. Portfolios, blogs, videos and such like replace the essay, the dissertation and the three-hour final examination. On some undergraduate programmes there are now no formal examinations. The result is grade inflation with more students getting upper second- and first-class degrees.

Predictability

'Predictability' in higher education involves the reconstruction of degree programmes so that they contain credit-bearing discrete modules with telephone directories full of 'learning objectives', 'learning outcomes', 'marking criteria' and 'level criteria'. The result is a highly structured training programme that students pass by meeting the desired outcomes.

Calculability

'Calculability' in higher education means *league tables*. Since Robin Wynyard and I first wrote about this topic they have gone from strength to strength. In 2003, a year after *The McDonaldization of Higher Education* appeared, the Shanghai Academic Ranking of World Universities (ARWU) was produced by the Shanghai Jiao Tong University. The Quacquarelli Symonds (QS) World University Rankings followed in 2004, produced in co-operation with the *Times Higher Education* (*THE*) until the latter went on to produce its own world rankings from 2010 onwards. As well as these there are many other rankings including various composite tables and those in the UK and elsewhere produced by newspapers such as the *Sunday Times*. Interestingly the *Guardian* produces a UK league table that ignores research. This is well thought of by lower ranking universities. The most prestigious, and financially rewarding, league table is the Research Assessment Exercise (RAE), now the Research Excellence Framework (REF). All of these tables can be broken down into regional and subject league tables. They will soon be joined by the Teaching Excellence Framework (TEF), discussed above.

The most influential of all league tables in the UK is the National Student Survey (NSS), which in its twelfth year (2016) showed an overall satisfaction rate of 86 per cent. The NSS can even be broken down to programme level, and this information is used by universities to seek improvements in teaching and often to discipline staff on programmes with low scores. Often students are rehearsed and bribed with Mars bars or the chance to win gifts to take part in the survey. Others fill the NSS forms in casually, unaware of the possible consequences for their lecturers.

The result is that no university can afford to ignore these tables, not merely because they are thought to, and are used to, influence student recruitment and retention but because any university that consistently comes at or towards the bottom of these tables might be put at risk of closure. Universities, therefore, have to spend an inordinate amount of time ensuring their position or trying to move up a few places on the growing number of league tables. We did not see the extent of the development of league tables of which this is a snapshot. Already there are plans to further develop the NSS, and the European Union has introduced the U-Multirank project, which 'puts less emphasis on reputation and allows students to select their own criteria to make comparisons' (Coughlan 2014).

Control

'Control' in higher education goes beyond annual appraisals or time-consuming monthly developmental review meetings which take place in all universities which monitor progress towards the achievement of targets. The worst aspect of the performance culture is what is known as Academic Workload Planning (AWP), the demotivating consequences of which have already been discussed. To recap, this is a popular, almost Stalinist, aspect of management in the post-1992 universities in the UK in which a lecturer's working year is deemed to consist of 1,600 or 1,650 hours (550 hours of teaching and the rest divided up between administration, curriculum development and research and scholarship). Every hour is accounted for. It is the crudest 'industrialisation' of the academic as worker as we saw above.

Other sources of control are less bureaucratic and more seductive because they emphasise professional 'development'. One is the universal attempt to get academics to achieve various levels of fellowship of the Higher Education Academy (HEA). The HEA was created out of the merger of the Institute for Learning and Teaching in Higher Education (ILTHE) and other bodies in 2003 as the nascent, member-led professional body for teachers in universities and colleges with the aim of enhancing the status of teaching. After several funding and other crises it is now essentially an undemocratic staff development body funded by universities promoting what its executive see as innovative learning and teaching methods. Initially, the HEA created a divide between newer lecturers who had to undertake mandatory teacher training courses and older, more experienced lecturers. That divide has diminished so that all 'lecturers' now focus on innovative 'student' or 'learner-centred' practice and teach to stated 'learning objectives'. One of the many things they learn in their training courses is how the 'lecture' that gives them their name is ineffective and even authoritarian.

Other forms of control that have developed recently are 'risk assessments' required by the Higher Education Funding Council for England (HEFCE) which runs its own assessment of universities at risk. These have created a climate of risk aversion in many institutions. In a similar but more ubiquitous way, the requirement to have all research – from first-year undergraduate projects to the work of inter-nationally acclaimed academics – approved by 'Ethics Committees' is introducing sclerosis into academia. Even thinking now has to be 'approved'.

The result of new forms of control is an acceptance of a student-centred approach to teaching 'learners' at the expense of the traditional role of the university in passing on the best that is known and thought to students. Worse still, students and society now need to be protected from any new knowledge that has not had prior 'approval' by a risk-averse Ethics Committee.

The McDonaldization paradox

A caveat has to be added at this point. In 1964 the Council for National Academic Awards (CNAA) was set up to ensure that degree courses validated by polytechnics and a variety of colleges were of a standard equivalent to that of universities. It was abolished by the Further and Higher Education Act of 1992 when the polytechnics became universities. At its peak the CNAA had approved undergraduate and postgraduate degree level courses in 140 institutions. This approval process was the model internalized by the new post-1992 universities and one which spread to almost all. I mention it as an attempt to maintain standards in a way that continues within universities today. McDonaldization has to be seen as a parallel process, as an attempt to maintain standards in an era of massification. It is not a process restricted to the UK but reflects a global problem of how to expand university education in countries like China and India. In the dozen years since our book came out, Robin Wynyard and I have talked many times to academic leaders from around the world and have expressed the challenge they face in the terms of a paradox:

> In an attempt to offer more students the benefits of higher education, the very processes introduced to achieve this and maintain quality undermine those benefits.

This is a problem that Ritzer has addressed as an example of the 'irrationality of rationality' but in a typically McDonaldized way, as reflects his role as the living embodiment of a single concept. He simply suggests inverting some of the features of McDonaldization and to 'deMcDonaldize' the university by making it 'inefficient', 'unpredictable', 'incalculable' (Ritzer 2002: 31). Ritzer says little about 'control', and apart from a newly found enthusiasm for 'non-human technology' his ideas are anecdotal and vague. In the end his inversion is just a clever trick, an attempt to wish away the reality of the McUniversity without attempting to understand its resonance with lecturers.

The McUniversity: just loving it!

Even this brief description of the bureaucratization of the contemporary British university may give the impression that McDonaldization has created the McUniversity. In conversation with us on visits, Ritzer himself was quite struck by the bureaucratization of the UK university.

It is tempting, following Ritzer (see Hayes 2005, 2013), to label the contemporary university the 'McUniversity' and describe it in the following way: The 'McUniversity' has come to be dominated by 'McManagers', who now constitute an ever-increasing percentage of university employees in the UK and US, with many whose role is said to be 'academic' also taking on time-consuming managerial roles and tasks (Ginsberg 2011; HESA 2014). 'McManagers' are heavily preoccupied with their universities' positions on ever-increasing numbers of 'league tables' and ensuring 'student satisfaction' for students paying up to £9,000 per annum in fees. They have to make sure they have trained 'McLecturers' who can teach easily digestible 'McLessons' to 'McStudents' who produce formulaic 'McEssays'. The idea that being an academic, particularly in a period of austerity, is being reduced to a deskilled and deprofessionalized 'McJob' with few intellectual demands and poor prospects has an obvious appeal to lecturers.

Much of this description will reflect the experience of many academics and students. For outsiders, here is a typical example of the 'McExperience' in the classroom. Students, having been taught in class that the aim is to achieve certain learning outcomes, are then asked to write essays with learning objectives. So they do. If they have to write a three-thousand-word essay with six learning objectives, they write five hundred words on each. The result is dull, formulaic writing. Their teachers then mark to the marking criteria developed from the learning objectives. If any are missing, the essay is marked down. There is no space for originality and creativity. Ask them to write an interesting essay and tell them that you will mark it to the criteria and they are often too afraid to do so. They are more comfortable writing to a formula. Students have become too scared to think for themselves, and most teachers are unwilling to take risks and make personal judgements when it means they may be challenged for not applying the correct marking criteria. It is best for both lecturers and students to leave work undemanding and their relationship cosy.

When Robin Wynyard and I first wrote about McUniversity we characterized the attitude of academics to McDonaldization as apathetic. Now it can only be seen as an attitude of acceptance. For some, particularly those promoting student-centred teaching and learning, the process of McDonaldization is nothing remarkable and, if anything, a positive development (see Rust 2008). The McUniversity just doesn't feel like a meat processing plant to faculty or to students. The reason is something Ritzer does not discuss – the rise of therapy culture.

Stress-free study: the therapeutic turn in higher education

I coined the term 'therapeutic university' to explain why the McUniversity was unchallenged. The existence of a therapeutic culture is well documented in sociological literature (see Nolan 1998; Furedi 2004; Ecclestone and Hayes 2008). It arose spontaneously to fill a political vacuum caused by the collapse of the traditional politics of left versus right in the 1990s. Left politics had always seen the working class as the subject of history and as an active agent in politics. In all its forms, from Stalinist communism to trade unionism, this agency vanished. Ordinary people were no longer seen as political agents but as potentially vulnerable or as victims. The new role of the state was not to contain working class struggle but offer therapy and counselling to victims (see Heartfield 2002).

In education, as elsewhere, this new state settlement in which politicians and professionals offered therapy to victims was an unhealthy development. Therapy is something you need when you are ill. Literally treating everyone as vulnerable did not empower the 'victims'; it empowered an army of professional and amateur therapists, many of them in teaching or support posts, to have a new view of their role.

Student counselling and courses to deal with 'stress' became commonplace. They were followed by warnings that certain courses may be disturbing and need 'trigger warnings' on course material and training on 'overcoming perfectionism' (Hayes 2014). Instead of going to university primarily to study subjects that might upset the vulnerable and fragile, universities have created something called the 'student experience' (see Mieschbuehler, Chapter 8 in this volume). The 'student experience' is an entirely new phenomenon. Not only does it mean that students now have their social life organized by universities but their academic life is made intellectually safe as well. 'Safe spaces' are allocated for debate and 'offensive' speech and 'offensive' speakers are banned. This 'cotton-wool' campus is the work of no single individual or organization; it is just natural to support these things in a therapeutic culture if you are not even aware of it and do not resist it.

The first step in challenging therapy culture is to realize that it is not antithetical to the meat processing vision that Ritzer presented of the McUniversity. It is complementary. The vulnerable need the support of the metaphorical 'iron cage' even if it is made up of bean bags but there is nothing soft about the new therapeutic culture. It is a new rigid orthodoxy. If you challenge it, you will be represented as being unfeeling and unsympathetic or even be seen as a victimizer.

But therapy culture in the therapeutic university must be challenged however difficult it is because it is ultimately dehumanizing. It facilitates an attack on the student as a human subject with extraordinary human potential and, by attacking subject knowledge, it reduces the student to someone who knows nothing but has the 'experiences' they are allowed to have. This dual attack on the human subject produces a diminished student self.

Ritzer's and many other people's concerns with combating McDonaldization remain abstract and are often no more than wishful thinking because they ignore therapy culture. Therapy culture does not create active human agents. It merely creates diminished individuals who seek more therapeutic experiences and, as I argue in Chapter 9, that is exactly what the Snowflake Generation will expect and demand.

The McDonaldization of the student soul

One danger of not challenging the therapeutic turn can be seen in the extension of the McDonaldizing process to the character and psychological makeup of individual students. Traditionally, students starting university might be excited about what they could become. They might want to be great thinkers, writers or scientists. But above all, they will want to be individuals. And this desire to be an individual, equipped with the knowledge and understanding needed to become critical and independent-minded, often means that students will dare to disagree and be different. Little wonder, then, that students can be challenging and difficult. This is not because they are encouraged by universities, under the banner of 'student voice', to express their feelings about things they know nothing about. No, students can be difficult and challenging because they have learned something about their academic subject and, on that basis, feel they can think independently, criticize and challenge. 'Dare to be different' might be a good slogan for any student.

But such a slogan would now probably be banned if it appeared on a T-shirt in many universities. That's because being an individual is now out and being a McDonaldized product with fixed 'graduate attributes' (GAs) is now in. In order to sell their graduate products to business, universities have drawn up lists of characteristics students must have acquired by the time they finish being processed.

This new and scary shift involves the McDonaldization of the student self. It's not just students' work that has to have 'outcomes'; the student soul now has to have outcomes, too, in the form of measurable 'attributes'.

The new GAs are all remarkably similar from institution to institution, either because they are all based on the model supplied by Australian universities, the originators of the phenomenon, or because they're the product of the same bureaucratic minds. Here are examples of GAs from RMIT University in Melbourne: work-ready, global in outlook and competence, environmentally aware and responsive, culturally and socially aware, innovative. Reading about them is a dispiriting experience. But you have to ask, as I'm sure any sensible employer will: 'What do RMIT students *know*?'

Similar GA outlines are already in place in many universities in the UK, but there is a general anxiety now about what they mean. Reading through lists of them on university websites, it is easy to see why. Some GAs are plucked from university courses, but others are pinched from particular subjects, which means that they quickly become meaningless without their original context. For example, what on earth is 'academic literacy'? It means what you want it to mean. Others appear to be therapeutic, such as 'critical self-awareness' or 'personal literacy'. The commonest – the requirement to be a 'global citizen' – is the emptiest of all. The explanation of what a global citizen is consists of fashionable buzzwords such as 'equity', 'social justice', 'sustainability' or 'diversity'. These bite-sized, easily digestible character nuggets are supposedly discovered through the intellectual rigour of campus focus groups. The real answer is that they probably came out of memories of personal, social and health education (PSHE) or citizenship classes in school and were adopted by academics and managers who see a university as nothing more than a big school.

New students should be aware that if they are in a GA university, lecturers will be organising their teaching so that they can ensure they are building the 'global citizen' with requisite 'personal literacy'. When the attributes involve academic subject knowledge or research skills the effect is not just absurd, it's damaging. They fragment subject knowledge and understanding into a set of bullet points severed from any particular discipline.

Any thoughtful individual might want to challenge the demand to support 'environmental concerns' and 'sustainability' rather than economic and social progress – or 'diversity' rather than universality. But such challenges require knowledge and understanding.

To enable any student to challenge the McDonaldization of their soul will involve a return to 'old-fashioned' academic work. The sociologists Richard Arum and Josipa Roksa have shown this to be the case (Arum and Roksa 2011, 2014). It is only by studying academic subjects, by reading and writing, that students learn to be critical, but this possibility is being undermined:

> Colleges and universities, not just students, have too often been academically adrift in recent decades ... both students and the schools they attend exist in larger structural and cultural contexts that have created the conditions under which the observed learning outcomes occur. Widespread cultural commitment to consumer choice and individual rights, self-fulfilment and sociability, and well-being and a broader therapeutic ethic leave little room for students or schools to embrace programs that promote academic rigor.
>
> *(Arum and Roksa 2014: 135–136)*

Beyond the McDonaldization of higher education

Although billions of McDonald's products are consumed every year, at the other extreme from the supposedly happy consumers are millions who hate what McDonald's stands for with a vengeance. McDonald's has been called the 'hate-brand of all time' (Toynbee 2000). This is not the case with the McUniversity, the daily reality of which is accepted even by those who write critiques of the marketization and commodification of higher education by managers and policy makers. I have argued that there are two reasons for this passivity – first, the lack of any political agency or any sense of human potential in wider society, and second, the seductions of therapy culture, which result in a contented passivity. This may seem a pessimistic and even fatalistic conclusion in line with Ritzer's general thinking about society. In conversation with me at the opening session of a conference on McDonaldization, George Ritzer described himself as 'more of a Weberian pessimist than a Marxist optimist' (see Hayes and Ritzer, Chapter 3 in this volume). I would like to take a more optimistic position as far as higher education is concerned by challenging the fatalism that the McDonaldization thesis encourages.

I have noted the general pessimism that Ritzer and Weber share about the way society is going; they also fear the loss of individuality with what Weber saw as the inexorable rise of bureaucracy and the rationality that went with it. As sociologists they both express concerns with the uniform movements of large numbers of people. However, Weber was always taking situations as *ideal types* which empirically could, as far as possible, be measured against what was out there in the real world. So what, for example, was bureaucracy for Weber only existed inasmuch as Prussia in the nineteenth century had a system of organization which approximated to it. Ritzer, on the other hand, wants to say that the world is becoming more and more McDonaldized, and it is his job as sociologist to prove it by finding more and more examples to substantiate the thesis. Along the steady march of McDonaldization there are hiccups caused by his 'irrationality of rationality', but these are mere peccadilloes which really don't alter things much. For Ritzer, disrupting the McDonaldized world is not only difficult but would also cause no end of problems.

What Ritzer's sociology does is more than describe. The examples he chooses, including the example of McDonald's, constitute a fatalistic ideology. But some examples can be given to show that McDonaldization and the therapeutic culture that complements it are not as all pervasive or inevitable as Ritzer thinks (see Hayes, Chapter 9 in this volume). But I want to end this introductory chapter on an optimistic statement on how to begin to de-McDonaldize the university.

Freedom of speech with that burger?

It came as a surprise to Greg Lukianoff, the president of the Foundation for Individual Rights in Education (FIRE), that defences of freedom of speech had become more noticeable recently, as Ceclia Capuzzi Simon said in a *New York Times* opinion piece:

> The free-speech watchdog FIRE is a familiar irritant to college administrators, but until this past year, the rest of the country wasn't paying much attention. An "epic" year is what Greg Lukianoff, president and chief executive of the Foundation for Individual Rights in Education, calls it. Colleges and universities were forced to publicly and painfully deal with a confluence of national issues – race, sexual assault, gay rights, politically correct speech – mirrored and magnified in the microcosm of campus life.
>
> *(Capuzzi Simon 2016)*

She considers part of the reason was the impact of the article he wrote with Jonathan Haidt for *The Atlantic,* 'The Coddling of the American Mind' (Lukianoff and Haidt 2015), in which they tackled the new, thin-skinned emotionalism on campus. They argued that

> Attempts to shield students from words, ideas, and people that might cause them emotional discomfort are bad for the students. They are bad for the workplace, which will be mired in unending litigation if student expectations of safety are carried forward. And they are bad for American democracy.
>
> *(Lukianoff and Haidt 2015)*

The belief that such emotional censorship is bad for universities and society is beginning to have more support (see Kissel, Chapter 6 in this volume). Increasing numbers of academics and young people simply do not want to be coddled. Here are some examples.

The campaign group Academics for Academic Freedom (AFAF) argues for freedom of speech with no 'ifs' and no 'buts' – even if it is deemed 'offensive'. It is growing in influence now that it is a membership organisation and undertakes case work in the UK the way FIRE does in the US.

But the most impressive campaigns for freedom of speech are those run by the undergraduates and recent graduates that gather around the UK on-line magazine *spiked*. One is the Free Speech Now! campaign. Another, the Down with Campus Censorship! campaign, targets 'No Platform' policies and practices as well as other restrictions on freedom of speech. This campaign is becoming a major challenge to the bureaucratic structures of universities, including student unions, all of whom censor and ban to protect 'vulnerable' students. More importantly, and ironically in the context of a paper on McDonaldization, are *spiked*'s Free Speech University Rankings (FSUR) launched in January 2015. As we have seen, universities love league tables, and since the rankings first appeared they have been forced to be aware of how they restrict free speech. In 2016 the FSUR revealed that 90 per cent of universities censor speech, up from 80 per cent in 2015, while 55 per cent had a hostile environment for freedom of speech. Although this is a bleak picture, the FSUR has made free speech, and with it academic freedom, a burning issue in the UK. Universities have to justify their censorship or seek to be less censorious.

I end by discussing freedom of speech because without that freedom the McUniversity cannot be challenged. The McDonaldization of higher education really applies to the bureaucratic superstructure of universities: management, student support services and student unions. Underneath these superstructures academics try to get on with their teaching and ignore what they can, from mission statements to puppy rooms. But as I illustrated by my opening examples, academics will be badly affected by the ongoing McDonaldizing processes. This paper is a wake-up call.

Critics of those destructive and disenchanting effects have found that they have to inform their academic colleagues and students about McDonaldization, and the complementary therapeutic aspects of the university, before they can be encouraged to challenge these effects.

Growing opposition to censorship and restrictions on free speech and academic freedom and to the infantilization of students are welcome signs that the therapeutic ethic that complements and supports McDonaldization is being challenged. We may be beginning to move beyond McUniversity.

Visions of higher education – about this book

When Robin Wynyard and I edited *The McDonaldization of Higher Education* we were interested in the analysing the concept, the McDonaldization process and its effects. (Although I never thought about it at the time, it probably was not a good career move to have that particular book title on my CV.) Similarly, the contributors to this book all wrote out of their intellectual curiosity about the possibility of going beyond McDonaldization.

The first two writers, Hayes and Poynter, show the destructive effects of McDonaldization on education and the university and how the present system must not and cannot continue. Hayes and Ritzer discuss whether Ritzer's pessimism about de-McDonaldization must prevail. Hayes believes it should not. Kennedy, Hornsby and Morello then discuss the possibility of creating a new university. Kennedy's vision is based on the Enlightenment, Hornsby and Morello's on a medieval vision of the liberal arts university with God at the centre. Kissel tackles growing censorship in America and argues for a Republic of Science separate from the state. Panton, Mieschbuehler and Hayes look at today's students. Panton discusses how sixth-form students can be challenged intellectually so they come to university with a passion for subject knowledge. Mieschbuehler provides a critique of how the 'student experience' has undermined knowledge-based education and presents a manifesto for moving beyond 'student experience'. Hayes explains the therapeutic turn in education and the challenges universities face now that the Snowflake Generation has matriculated. Finally, Williams, writing from China, offers his thoughts on how China can go beyond McDonaldization and develop independent critical and creative thinkers.

The authors in this book are speaking out. How the world will receive their ideas is uncertain, and that is what makes this book exciting.

Note

1 Sections of this chapter draw upon and update Hayes, D. and Wynyard, R. (2016), The McDonaldization of higher education revisited, in Côté, J. and Furlong, A. (eds.) *The Routledge Handbook of the Sociology of Higher Education*, London and New York: Routledge.

References

Academics for Academic Freedom (AFAF): www.afaf.org.uk.

Arum, R. and Roksa, J. (2011) *Academically Adrift: Limited Learning on College Campuses*, Chicago and London: The University of Chicago Press.

Arum, R. and Roksa, J. (2014) *Aspiring Adults Adrift: Tentative Destinations of College Graduates*, Chicago and London: The University of Chicago Press.

Bloomberg News (2011) Getting into Harvard easier than McDonald's university in China, 26 September: http://www.bloomberg.com/news/2011-01-26/getting-into-harvard-easier-than-mcdonald-s-hamburger-university-in-china.html (accessed 2 August 2016).

Capuzzi Simon, C. (2016) Fighting for free speech on America's campuses, *New York Times*, 1 August: http://www.nytimes.com/2016/08/07/education/edlife/fire-first-amendment-on-campus-free-speech.html?_r=0 (accessed 19 August 2016).

Chalabi, M. and Burn-Murdoch, J. (2013) McDonald's 34,492 restaurants: where are they? *Guardian*, 17 July: http://www.theguardian.com/news/datablog/2013/jul/17/mcdonalds-restaurants-where-are-they (accessed 26 September 2014).

Coughlan, S. (2014) What makes a global top 10 university? BBC News, 16 September: http://www.bbc.co.uk/news/business-29086590 (accessed 26 September 2014).

Economist (2013) Fries with that? A degree in burgerology and a job too, 27 April: http://www.economist.com/news/international/21576656-degree-burgerologyand-job-too-fries (accessed 26 September 2014).

Ecclestone, K. and Hayes, D. (2008) *The Dangerous Rise of Therapeutic Education*, Abingdon, Oxon, and New York, NY: Routledge.

Epstein, E. A. (2012) Chew on this: Inside McDonald's Hamburger University – the 'Harvard of the fast food biz', *Daily Mail*, 12 April: http://www.dailymail.co.uk/news/article-2128250/Chew-A-peek-inside-McDonalds-Hamburger-University-delicious-school-world.html#ixzz3EcadYBGE (accessed 26 September 2014).

Foundation for Individual Rights in Education (FIRE): http://www.thefire.org/.

Free Speech Now!: http://www.spiked-online.com/freespeechnow.

Free Speech University Rankings: http://www.spiked-online.com/free-speech-university-rankings#.V74LgZgrLIU.

Furedi, F. (2004) *Therapy Culture: Cultivating Vulnerability in an Uncertain Age*, Abingdon, Oxon, and New York, NY: Routledge.

Ginsberg, B. (2011) Administrators ate my tuition, *Washington Monthly*, September/October: http://www.washingtonmonthly.com/magazine/septemberoctober_2011/features/administrators_ate_my_tuition031641.php?page=all (accessed 26 September 2014).

Hayes, D. (2002) The new sophistry of teacher training for higher education, in Hayes, D. and Wynyard, R. (eds.) *The McDonaldization of Higher Education*, Westport, CT, and London: Bergin and Garvey: 143–158.

Hayes, D. (2005) Diploma? Is that with fries? *Times Educational Supplement*, 10 June: http://www.tes.co.uk/article.aspx?storycode=2108523 (accessed 26 September 2014).

Hayes, D. (2013) The McDonaldization of the student soul, spiked, 3 October: http://www.spiked-online.com/newsite/article/the_mcdonaldisation_of_the_student_soul/14105#.VEpe6vldWM4 (accessed 26 September 2014).

Hayes, D. (2014) How trigger warnings shoot down free debate, spiked, 20 March: http://www.spiked-online.com/newsite/article/how-trigger-warnings-shoot-down-free-debate/14816#.VE5skqFFDcs (accessed 26 September 2014).

Hayes, D. and Wynyard, R. (eds.) (2002) *The McDonaldization of Higher Education*, Westport, CT, and London: Bergin and Garvey.

Hayes, D. and Wynyard, R. (2016) The McDonaldization of higher education revisited, in Côté, J. and Furlong, A. (eds.) *The Routledge Handbook of the Sociology of Higher Education*, Abingdon, Oxon, and New York, NY: Routledge.

Heartfield, J. (2002) *The 'Death of the Subject' Explained*, Sheffield, UK: Sheffield Hallam University Press.

HESA (2014) Staff in higher education institutions, Cheltenham, UK: Higher Education Statistics Agency: https://www.hesa.ac.uk/stats-staff (accessed 26 September 2014).

House of Commons Business, Innovation and Skills Committee (2016) *The Teaching Excellence Framework: Assessing Quality in Higher Education*, London: The Stationery Office Ltd: www.publications.parliament.uk/pa/cm201516/cmselect/cmbis/572/572.pdf   (accessed 11 August 2016).

Johnson, D. (2013) McDouble is 'cheapest and most nutritious food in human history', *Telegraph*, 30 July: http://www.telegraph.co.uk/foodanddrink/10210327/McDouble-is-cheapest-and-most-nutritious-food-in-human-history.html (accessed 20 August 2016).

Lukianoff, G. and Haidt, J. (2015) The coddling of the American mind, *The Atlantic*, September: http://www.theatlantic.com/magazine/archive/2015/09/the-coddling-of-the-american-mind/399356/ (accessed 19 August 2016).

McDonald's (2014) *McDonalds.com*, https://www.mcdonalds.com/us/en-us.html (accessed 1 November 2014)

Margolis, E. (2013) The changing hidden curriculum: a personal recollection, in DeVitis, J. L. (ed.) *Contemporary Colleges and Universities: A Reader*, New York, NY: Peter Lang Publishing: 242–262.

Nolan, J. (1998) *The Therapeutic State: Justifying Government at Century's End*, New York, NY: New York University Press.

Ritzer, G. (1983) The McDonaldization of society, *Journal of American Culture*, 6(1): 100–107.

Ritzer, G. (1993) *The McDonaldization of Society*, Thousand Oaks, CA: Pine Forge Press.

Ritzer, G. (2000) *The McDonaldization of Society* (New Century Edition), Thousand Oaks, CA: Pine Forge Press.

Ritzer, G. (2002) Enchanting McUniversity: towards a spectacularly irrational university quotidian, in Hayes, D. and Wynyard, R. (eds.) *The McDonaldization of Higher Education*, Westport, CT and London: Bergin and Garvey.

Ritzer, G. (2008) *The McDonaldization of Society* (Fifth Edition), Thousand Oaks, CA: Pine Forge Press.

Ritzer, G. (2002, 2009) *McDonaldization: The Reader*, Thousand Oaks, CA: Pine Forge Press.

Rust, C. (2008) Food for thought – but where's the meat? *Teaching News*, Oxford Brookes University (Autumn) 20 November: https://ewiki.brookes.ac.uk/pages/viewpage.action?pageId=14131430 (accessed 26 September 2014).

Telegraph (2010) McDonald's opens Hamburger University in Shanghai, 30 March: http://www.telegraph.co.uk/news/worldnews/asia/china/7537573/McDonalds-opens-Hamburger-University-in-Shanghai.html (accessed 26 September 2014).

Weber, M. (1930) *The Protestant Ethic and the Spirit of Capitalism*, London: Allen and Unwin.

2

BEYOND INSTRUMENTALISM

Why education is living on borrowed time

Gavin Poynter

Introduction

Education has been cast as a cause of and saviour from the long depression that has afflicted the West since the 1970s. Governments have criticized those who teach, what has been taught and the achievement levels of students, whether it be in schools, colleges or universities. Reform has begot reform, with each phase used to assert and reassert education's instrumental purpose in helping generate a creative dynamism in societies such as the USA and UK. Two decades into the twenty-first century, this goal remains elusive.

Since the 1970s, in the USA and Britain, a significant expansion of post-compulsory education provision has accompanied the narrowing of the prevailing view of its purpose. Prior to its massification, for example, university provided the vehicle for the education and professional development of a civic, commercial and political elite. Its public purpose, whether funded privately or by the state, was implicit if not always openly expressed. The rapid state-supported expansion of the sector strengthened its claim to be a public good – a benefit to society that extends beyond the individual recipient of the education itself. But, paradoxically, widened participation has witnessed its erosion.

For many critics, the main cause of this erosion has been education's marketization. But the argument presented here suggests that this narrative, adopted albeit for different purposes by governments and critics alike, does less than justice to the centrality of the state in the transformation of education in contemporary society. The two nations most closely identified with the ideologies of the market – the USA and Britain – are used to illustrate how the state has used the sector to mitigate and contain the effects of an unprecedentedly long depression. Rather than its subordination to the exigencies of market relations, education has assumed a significant role in sustaining a stagnant social and economic order.

The chapter divides into four sections. First, the changing emphases of intervention from containing and managing the effects of the recessions of the 1970s and early 1980s through to the state-driven process of financialization in the late twentieth and early twenty-first century are outlined. Secondly, the impact of these trends on compulsory and post-compulsory education in the United States and Britain are discussed. Despite the financial pressures on the state, public spending on education as a proportion of total expenditure in both countries has risen while at the same time the sector has created opportunities for capital to offer an increasingly diverse provision of education services. This creeping privatisation has provided new market opportunities for private enterprise. But more significantly it has facilitated the dissemination of a target-oriented managerialism across the sector as a whole and is illustrative of a broader economic trend, of capital's seeking of relatively low-risk opportunities for profit making via its growing dependency on contractual relations with the state.

Thirdly, it is argued that financialization has witnessed the emergence within the education system of what is called the subprime student arising from the expansion of the state-supported student loan system in both nations. The rapid expansion of loan provision strengthens the perception of learning as a mere transaction between teachers and taught and, while debt levels are not comparable to those achieved prior to the US property market crash in 2007–8, they are symbolic of the degradation of education's role and standing in contemporary society. The final section suggests that these reforms – coupled with the instrumentalism to which education has been relentlessly submitted over the course of the long depression, has left the sector in a precarious condition. Now, from school to university – education is conceived as a private asset, the very antithesis of its potential as a public good.

State intervention: from managing progress to containing crises

There is a broad consensus amongst economists that the growth rates of the economies of the advanced Western nations have significantly slowed since the 1970s. There is less agreement about the underlying causes of the slowdown. In the initial phase of the long depression,[1] some economists highlighted exogenous factors, such as rapid and unexpected changes in oil prices, others the barriers to increased productivity arising from domestic conditions such as the growth in the public sector and in employment associated with nonmarket outputs (Bacon and Eltis 1976).

More recent and reflective arguments have focused upon the structural – the exhaustion of the second industrial revolution of technological innovation that, for the esteemed American economic historian, Robert Gordon, lasted in the USA between 1870 and 1970. The third revolution – the emergence of the digital age – is unlikely to have an equivalent impact (Gordon 2016). Though Gordon is a highly respected economist, what critics identify as his techno-pessimism has been countered by those who argue that a new age is just around the corner – that the digital revolution is about to create the conditions for future abundance (Mokyr 2013).

Others acknowledge recent advances in technology but reach opposite conclusions about the implications for society: some may enjoy an abundance of material wealth while the majority will be poor and jobless (Castells 2001; Susskind and Susskind 2015).

Left economists have also focused upon structural conditions and in particular the underlying tendency of the rate of profit to fall in the advanced Western economies, tracing the decline back to the late 1960s and early 1970s in the UK and USA and a little later in other nations such as Germany and Japan (Bullock and Yaffe 1974; Clarke 1994; Brenner 2002; Kliman 2014). Offsetting this decline, according to the critics, has been a process of globalisation of production, the rise of financial capital and the emergence of a market-oriented capitalism in which the inequalities of wealth distribution are a central feature. For the critics of what is widely called a neo-liberal order, 'unleashed', and 'rampant' capitalism (Gamble 2009; Glyn 2006; Hall 2000; Harvey 2007) has characteristically experienced a series of crises, the latest in 2007–8 being the most profound. Though there are many different strands to the left critique of neo-liberalism, from Keynesian, Heterodox, post-Keynesian and Marxian, they tend to share a common view that the state in Western nations has subordinated its role to the market and market relations – the opposite of the view developed here. Below it is argued that the state-led processes of mitigation, containment and financialization have been essential to sustaining an undynamic economic order in which many private enterprises have become increasingly dependent upon the state for their survival.

Significant changes took place in the West's political elites' perception of the role of the state over the course of the long depression, from 'guiding progress' during the postwar boom years to containing crisis between the mid-70s to early 1990s in the UK and USA and, finally, to affirming capital's increasing state-dependency in the aftermath of the financial crisis of 2007–8. Each successive phase witnessed a growing loss of confidence within the elites in their capacity to sustain material progress to the extent that it is now widely accepted that future generations will not secure the kind of improvements in their standards of living that previous generations have enjoyed.

Each of these phases affirm an historic lesson that the state over the past century in all Western economies has performed an increasingly essential role in economic affairs even when it has been in the hands of governments ideologically committed to its withdrawal. The transitions in each country had their own specific cultural, political and institutional characteristics. Each sustained elements of the 'old' alongside the adoption of 'new' forms of intervention. The balance between the two shifted toward the latter as crises recurred in the early 1990s, then in 2000 and reached their most acute form with the credit crunch that commenced 2007–8.

Harold Wilson, as leader of the Labour Party in Britain, in 1963 captured the optimism associated with state intervention during the golden age in his call to harness science and the new technologies to meet society's needs in his 'white heat' speech to the Labour Party conference in 1963: 'The conscious purposive use of scientific progress' could provide 'undreamed of living standards and the possibility of leisure ultimately on an unbelievable scale' (Wilson 1963:3). The state was essential to the planning and delivery of such a future, and education, broadly delivered via general taxation, underpinned prospects for sustaining a cohesive social order that replaced the discord of the earlier decades of the twentieth century and enabled political leaders to proclaim the superiority of Western democracy over the Soviet system. US hegemony underpinned Western capitalism. It provided exchange rate certainty (through the Bretton Woods system), and investment in Western Europe and Japan secured American profitability, raising fixed capital formation in the recipient nations and their access to advanced US technologies. The result was strong productivity growth, though there were signs of this slowing in the UK and USA in the late 1960s.

The end of the golden age was reflected in the weakening of confidence, particularly evident in the UK and USA, in the progressive nature of state intervention. The initial phase of the long recession witnessed attempts by successive administrations to contain the impacts of the loss of productive dynamism – to adapt the state's role to one of mitigating the effects of a cyclical downturn that impacted severely on manufacturing and other traditional industries. While the underlying cause of the end of the golden age was falling profitability relative to that which is required to fund a new round of productivity-enhancing capital investment, the specific trigger was the problem of the US dollar's role as the world's reserve currency.

When President Nixon ended the Bretton Woods agreement in August 1971, refusing to redeem dollars for gold and ending the fixed exchange between the two, the dollar's role as the world's reserve relied upon the confidence of its traders in the US's continued economic supremacy. The dollar's value was determined by the US Treasury and Federal Reserve, it became as Engdahl has noted a 'political currency' (Engdahl 2006) against which other currencies floated, laying the foundations for the deregulation of financial markets and requiring nations to hold dollar reserves (the source of the rise in the Eurodollar market). A huge shock to this arrangement occurred with the rise in oil prices (by 400 per cent) in 1973 and 1975. Oil was traded in dollars, the US move away from the fixed exchange with gold had led to its devaluation, and the oil price hike was prompted by the OPEC nations' attempt to compensate for the fall in the value of the dollar. The consequence was a rapid fall in stock market values, and recession hit all the western economies.

State intervention in the West's advanced economies shifted toward containment with responses that alternated between curbing inflation and providing a stimulus through increased government spending. The US government responded belatedly to the crisis in 1975, by shifting focus from tackling inflation to providing an economic stimulus via increased government expenditure in areas like education, health and welfare. In turn, the education and welfare systems put in place during the golden years shifted in their conception and purpose in the 1970s from being broadly based on ideas of citizenship, social justice and social inclusion to adjusting to the breakdown of the industrial order of the golden age.

A key feature of the containment phase was the overall rise in public expenditure (in Japan 19.3 per cent of GDP in 1970 to 32.2 per cent in 1980; across Europe from 38 per cent in 1967 to 46 per cent in 1976; and in the US from 25 per cent in 1966 to 32 per cent in 1982). The effect, as Mattick (2011) has noted, was a 'rapid infusion of cash in the economy ... government funds limit[ed] the effects of the downturn'. And as Minsky observed, the huge stimulus provided by government spending in the US (and elsewhere) helped sustain corporate profitability even in the mid-1970s (Minsky 1986:10). Extensive rationalisation took place but not to the extent that capital assets were written down and the conditions for a new round of accumulation laid; government intervention moderated the crisis but also limited the extent of its recovery. The huge injection of credit into the world's economy in the mid-1970s, combined with the first phases of the deregulation of financial markets, created the conditions for the state-led process of financialization.

The significant role of finance arose from the decline of the West's productive dynamism and was an outcome of that decline. The injection of credit or easy money into the world's economy was a central feature, a product of the acts of central banks and indicative of their increasing importance since the mid-1970s. The state's role in supporting financialization was especially evident in the USA and Britain, not least via the regulatory reforms that reduced the restrictions on what banks could do through the Big Bang reforms of banking in the UK in 1985–6 and the repeal of the Glass/Steagall Act in the USA in 1999. Its main characteristic, however, was the shift toward assisting capital to offset rather than address the underlying causes of productive decline. The story of the rise of finance capital starts, counterintuitively, not with the financial sector but with nonfinancial enterprises and is illustrated best by reference to the USA.

In the 1974–5 and 1980–1 recessions, government deficits grew dramatically; corporate investment fell but corporate profits increased as a result of the injection of money by the state into the US economy. In the 1980s nonfinancial enterprises used their money surpluses not to enhance their productive capacity but to seek new market opportunities through mergers and acquisitions, and they also turned to securities markets rather than banks to fund their activities. Mergers and acquisitions were effective ways of raising stock values well in excess of the underlying or real values of the companies that were reconfigured. In turn, restructuring was facilitated by the state through deregulation, a process that began under President Carter in 1978 with industry-specific deregulation achieved by 1982 in banking, broadcasting, communications, transportation and oil and gas. It was in these industries that mergers were most prevalent (35 per cent by total asset value between 1981 and 1986). The merger and acquisitions boom 'shaded into a larger pattern of speculation in financial markets rather than investing in productive enterprises' (Mattick 2011:60). Speculation expanded with the introduction of new financial instruments – derivatives, swaps, securities (Poynter 2012).

State support for financialization was considerably strengthened by the expansion of credit and the adoption of policies favourable, particularly in the USA and UK, to increasing household or personal debt especially via the provision of mortgages in the property market. On the one hand, personal borrowing to secure housing (and compensate for wage stagnation) increased significantly, while on the other (savings), the reform of pension schemes, shifting progressively from public to private provision, generated a significant increase in the role of pension funds as sources of institutional investment in stock markets. These trends in household borrowing and savings were not replicated evenly across the Western economies (Lapavitsas 2013:243–5) but did eventually culminate in the credit bubble in the US housing market setting off the 2007–8 crisis.

State-sponsored financialization did much to hide the long decline in productive investment. The camouflage had several features evident to different degrees in each Western society. Centrally, easy credit, regulatory reforms and the increase in financial flows from emerging economies to those such as the USA and Britain allowed the latter to hold persistent trade and current account deficits, in effect to live beyond their means. At the same time, state-induced flexibility in domestic labour markets supported employers' cost cutting and the re-ordering of education and welfare provision through increased use of contracted services generated profitable, relatively low-risk opportunities for private capital. This was accompanied by government stepping back from direct intervention as central banks and 'technocratic', quasi-state or arms-length agencies assumed an increasing presence in the regulation of domestic affairs.

The camouflage slipped in the wake of the credit crunch. The last decade has witnessed intervention on an unprecedented scale, supporting capital and, in turn increasing its dependency on the state. Dependency has assumed several dimensions. First, bailout and tax relief programmes for corporations have increased significantly over the past decade in the USA and Britain. Secondly, the state (and in the European context, the European Central Bank) has adopted new monetary measures (quantitative easing) that have boosted bank balance sheets in an attempt to stimulate increased business confidence. Thirdly, these support measures have generated a significant rise over 2008–16 in general government debt. Finally, there has been a growth in the contracting of private capital to undertake public service provision, particularly in sectors such as education while, at the same time, the state has sought to increasingly shift the cost of post-compulsory education and training provision toward the household or the private 'consumer' of its provision.

The changing role of education

Over the course of the long depression, the fortunes of the education sector have reflected the broader trends outlined above. In the golden age, education was conceived in progressive societal terms – President Johnson's Great Society initiative perceived education as essential to providing opportunities to all. Federal aid for education increased, and Head Start was but one initiative designed to provide enhanced learning opportunities for socially disadvantaged students. In the UK, in the late 1960s, new universities were created and secondary education reformed. The abolition (albeit piecemeal across Local Education Authorities) of the selection process to UK secondary schools facilitated the introduction of comprehensives in the late 1960s and '70s and reflected a commitment to education as a means of enhancing social mobility and equality of opportunity. The progressive ethos waned (or more accurately was reinterpreted) in the course of the subsequent two decades. Influenced by the 'fallacies'[2] of human capital theory that accords the pursuit of economic gain as a foundation of peoples' actions, education and particularly training policy was increasingly utilized by successive governments in their attempts to manage the social and economic effects of the 1970s downturn.[3]

In the USA, the need for education reform was associated with the nation's weakening economic performance and the competitive challenge presented by nations such as Japan. This concern was reflected in the influential 1983 report *A Nation at Risk,* produced by the federal government supported National Commission for Education Excellence (Finegold, McPharland and Richardson 1993). In the UK, successive Conservative governments (1979–97) conducted reforms in UK education and training provision that were, in turn, influenced by those previously introduced in the USA. The UK's Training and Enterprise Councils (TECs), introduced in 1988, for example, drew heavily for their inspiration upon the USA's Private Industry Councils (PICS) (Bailey 1993:7).

In short, approaches to the reform of education and training provision reflected increasing concerns in both nations about the de-industrialising effects of the recessions of the 1970s and early 1980s and the social disruption, particularly the rise in youth unemployment that accompanied them. And in each, the education system was seen as symptomatic of that decline and its reform a means to contain it. From the early 1980s, in the UK, educational standards in schools drew considerable criticism from members of the newly elected Conservative government, despite the lack of evidence of their decline over the preceding decade (see Tomlinson 2011:26 and the Green Paper *Education in Schools* produced by the Department of Education and Science in 1977). Schooling became one of the scapegoats for the wider social malaise arising from the UK's experience of the first decade of the long depression. For the Conservative government, the reform of education was associated with the restoration of 'traditional' values of individual achievement with local authority powers over its provision much diminished.

Training programmes were also redesigned, their reform commencing in the mid-1970s with the adoption of schemes designed to address the dramatic rise in youth unemployment. The school leaving age was raised from 15 to 16 years in 1972 and Youth Training Schemes introduced whose numbers increased from 10,000 in 1974 to 240,000 by 1977. The steep rise (see Table 2.1) was indicative of a decisive shift from the perception of training being associated with learning a specific profession, skill or occupation to becoming a vehicle for containing or mitigating the social impacts of economic decline.[4]

Since this initial phase of the long recession, reform has begot reform. Paradoxically, as the ideology of market disciplines, espoused by successive governments, has been adopted widely within the sector, the involvement of and cost to the state of compulsory and post-compulsory education (as a proportion of total public expenditure in both the USA and Britain) has risen.

TABLE 2.1 Learners at FE institutions, England and Wales, 1960–2010 (thousands)

Year	Total (FT/PT/Evening)
1960	2,229
1970	3,115
1980	3,343
1990	3,871
2000	4,444
2010	4,265

Source: Author's, drawn from Bolton, P. (2012) Education: Historical Statistics Standard Note: SN/SG/4252 House of Commons Library, November.

The financialization of education

The most recent phase of the long depression, characterized by financialization, has witnessed attempts to contain the cost of post-compulsory education by shifting responsibility from state funding to households or individual loans. This has created an unprecedented rise in student debt and considerable concern in both nations about debt default. Continuing reform of school education has involved publicly funded private and charitable institutions in the management and running of schools and a diminished role for local states/authorities.

The dilution of local state provision has arisen, in part, from the presumption that consumer or parental choice plays a significant part in creating competition between schools for the enrolment of pupils and introducing this quasi-market orientation enhances school performance and student achievement. There is evidence from the UK that where there is competition within specific, often urban, localities, a segregation based on educational abilities is accentuated between schools, a trend that tends to strengthen social polarization and the idea of education as a private rather than community-based asset.[5] This latest phase, involving the melding of public and private institutions has, despite the increased diversity of public and private providers, given considerable impetus to the state's role in the shaping of education and training as a brief review of school, vocational and higher education provision in the USA and Britain reveals.

Compulsory schooling

In the USA the trend toward consumer/parental choice has been reflected in the emergence of various forms of Education Management Organisations (EMOs), including charter schools and the growth of a diverse range of private school voucher schemes adopted by states and localities. By 2013, over 40 states had passed legislation approving charter schools, and there were 6,400 in operation with 2.3 million enrolments (rising from 0.3 million in 1999). The schools are state funded, though the majority engage in extensive private fund raising activities. Contractually, staff are private sector employees of the EMO that runs the school. By 2013, there were about 115,000 teachers and approximately 30,000 support staff employed by charter schools, about 3.5 percent of the total number of teachers in the USA (US Department of Education 2013). Public funding of private schools occurs in the USA through the voucher system and scholarships (often provided to disadvantaged communities) and government support for faith-based schools. It is estimated that about 19 states offer one or both of these and that around 220,000 school students were recipients of scholarship awards in 2012.

A similar trend toward the melding of the public and private has taken place in the UK education sector. In his analysis, Stephen Ball referred to the role of the state as a 'market maker' in 'the managed development of school privatisation' (Ball 2007:38) with the process involving the large scale, such as Public Private Finance (PFI) initiatives to construct new schools as well as the relatively smaller scale provision of a range of services, including IT, supply teachers, school meals and specialist learning support services. In the decade since Ball's analysis, the process he described has accelerated across all parts of the education sector.

The private sector's role in education service delivery (rather than capital spending on infrastructure) is illustrated by Babcock Education, a subsidiary of the company mostly known for its vast nuclear, defence, engineering and construction activities. It is also 'the UK's largest integrated education improvement and support services provider and we work with schools, academies, multi-academy trusts, teaching school alliances, UTCs, local authorities and government departments (Babcock 2016). It employs 600 staff 'to provide consultancy, training and management services to more than 50 UK local authorities'. With Devon Council, for example, in 2012 it secured a £125 million, seven-year contract to supply 'education and inclusion support and improvement services' to the county's schools and education service (Babcock:ibid.).

A further illustration of the melding of the public and private in the UK is indicated by the broad equivalent of the USA's charter school movement: the academy schools. Introduced by a Labour government in 2002 (to raise standards in failing schools), they were subsequently promoted by the coalition government (2010–15) and the Conservative government (2015-present) for whom the compulsory conversion of all secondary schools to academy status was proposed in early 2016, though the compulsory element was withdrawn by May 2016 in the face of considerable opposition, not least from within the Conservative Party itself. The academy school is directly funded by national government and may be newly established or may have converted from local to central government funding and control. The academy is run by a charitable body and may be part of a chain of charitable trusts; other types of schools (free schools and University Technology Colleges) also have academy status. Teaching staff remain public sector employees, contracted to the state rather than a local authority.

The relationship with the private sector is through the establishment of the trust itself and via the procurement of services by the academy or chain of trusts. Several have been criticized for purchasing services from their own trust board members and executives. In 2014, for example, the *Daily Telegraph* newspaper reported that nine academy trust chains had paid millions of pounds to companies with private links to board members and trust senior management, including the largest chain, Academies Enterprise Trust, and the Grace Academy, which 'paid more than £1 million either directly to or through companies controlled by its founder Lord Edmiston, trustees' relatives or to the board of trustees. The trust, which runs three schools in the Midlands, made payments including £533,789 to International Motors Limited, a company owned by the Conservative donor' (Dixon 2014). The Collaborative Academies Trust was established by the American-owned company Edison Learning UK. It runs seven academies and a total of 26 schools and provides other educational services to around 400 schools in England. According to the trust's annual report and accounts for 2014–15, its income from the schools it runs was £16.9 million, excluding capital funding (Collaborative Academies Trust 2015).

Procurement of other services by all schools – from supply teachers to IT and school dinners – has increased significantly over the last decade. Of the little under £40 billion spent on primary and secondary schools in 2014–15, about 20 per cent was spent on services. A significant proportion of this was on procurement from the private sector. For example, around 44,000 supply teachers work each week in schools, accounting for an expenditure of £1.3 billion in 2014–15 with over half provided by about 150 private sector agencies (Whittaker 2015). Serco, the management services company, had a turnover of £140 million from education services, including Ofsted inspections, education department contracts, and providing services such as curriculum development, leadership and management benchmarking to 330 schools (TUC 2014:2).

Charitable trust status thinly obscures the involvement of subsidiaries of companies historically associated with industrial production (e.g., Babcock, Vosper Thorneycroft Education and Edison). Such companies are currently engaged in merger and acquisition activities. In its report, published in spring 2014, Catalyst Corporate Finance reported that within the private sector:

> The pace of M&A activity is being supported by increasing private sector involvement in the delivery of education services, rising global demand for education and higher expectations of attainment in a competitive world economy. A scarcity of assets is driving high valuations for quality assets.
>
> *(Catalyst Corporate Finance 2014:1)*

Characteristics of financialized capitalism via public/private partnerships in the funding of infrastructure,[6] the melding of public and private sectors in service delivery, and the growth of merger and acquisition activities are now commonplace in the UK schools sector with the UK emulating many of the trends evident in the USA. The private sector provides an expanding range of services, reflecting the proliferation in the types of schools and their management structures.

Training and vocational education

Training and vocational education in the UK has experienced a series of reforms since the mid-1970s, the most recent providing, according to government perspectives, greater autonomy to colleges and private sector providers. Though autonomy has carried with it a considerable degree of central government intervention in the form of performance targets and regulation (Hodgson 2015). The sector is complex, and its colleges have experienced major funding issues since 2010. The sector's problems reflect the wider malaise within the UK's economy (and the USA's) – an hourglass labour market that divides into high- and low-skilled jobs with little in between. In turn, this creates significant problems for a sector whose main purpose is vocational education that provides intermediate skills.

In the UK the growth in provision has been boosted by private training agencies competing for skills-based training programmes supported by public funding managed from 2001 until its closure in 2008 by the quasi-state agency the Learning and Skills Council (LSC). While the main providers of LSC-supported education and training were FE colleges and sixth form centres (409 UK institutions), the LSC registered 1548 business organisations and 214 voluntary organisations as providers of training courses supported by LSC funding in November 2005. By 2010, the LSC had been replaced by two agencies: the Education Funding Agency (EFA) and the Skills Funding Agency (SFA). The EFA is responsible for funding for schools, academies and other elements of the work of the Department of Education; it provided over £50 billion to schools, academies and colleges in 2012–13. This spend was primarily upon public sector educational provision. By 2012, employees in English FE colleges were reclassified as being in the private sector (a total of 200,000 jobs transferred), though their funding remained overwhelmingly from the EFA and SFA. The SFA is overseen by the Department of Business, Innovation and Skills. The combined budget for all FE provision in 2015 was £7 billion (NAO 2015).

The Association of Employment and Learning Providers, the main trade association in the sector, claimed over 670 members in 2015, including private companies and public not-for-profit organisations. In 2014, the National Audit Office report on the financial sustainability of the FE sector estimated that '[i]n England, there are around 1,100 providers, including around 240 FE colleges delivering education and training to more than half of the sector's learners. Around 700 providers are commercial or charitable bodies, supporting most of the remaining learners' (NAO:ibid.).

In the USA, vocational education and training provision is referred to as career and technical education (CTE), a rebranding designed to improve its social standing. The federal government framework for CTE provision was established by the 1998 Workforce Investment Act (WIA) and the Carl D. Perkins Career and Technical Education and Improvement Act of 2006 (Perkins IV). Both acts arose from widely held concerns over the inadequacy and inconsistency of provision across states in the USA. CTE is delivered through a devolved system that, despite the reforms introduced by the acts, an OECD study described in the most unflattering terms:

> In international perspective, perhaps the most striking feature of the US approach to postsecondary CTE is the very high degree of decentralization, with multiple foci of governance and policy development. ... In the US educational system, decentralization is ubiquitous, in diverse relatively autonomous institutions and multiple accreditation bodies, in the lack of national skills or occupational standards, in the deregulated array of industry certifications, in the substantial role of the private for-profit sector in delivering training provision, in the limited role of employers and unions acting collectively to shape provision, either at national or state level, and in the most deregulated labor market in the OECD. Even in comparison with countries, such as the UK and Australia, which share some characteristics with the US, the US stands at an extreme end in a spectrum of decentralization.
>
> *(OECD 2013)*

In the wake of the financial crisis, over the last decade federal funding of CTE has broadly risen whilst that provided by states has declined. Public (community colleges) and private (for-profit and not-for-profit) institutions offer CTE courses which are typically one of two types: postsecondary certificates focused on occupational skills, which are up to two years in length (see Table 2.2), and associate degrees, two-year degrees that are either academic or occupational. Community colleges account for a significant proportion of the associate degree provision while for-profit institutions focus primarily upon two-year certificate courses, providing around half of the total. The course awards are referred to as credentials, and in each year around 1.5 million are awarded, the most popular being in health care.

Since the 1960s, higher education in the USA has been paid for by a combination of grants and loans. The system of federal provision of need-based grants and loans was extended to vocational/community colleges by the Higher Education Act of 1972. Over the course of subsequent decades, legislative reforms supported an increase in loans alongside the relative reduction in the value of grants as the cost of educational provision itself increased. By the end of the first decade of the twenty-first century, federal and state support reached a 30-year low. Under the Obama administration, the federal government took steps to curb the rise in student debt and required public and for-profit education providers, in order to qualify for federal student aid, to prepare students for 'gainful employment in a recognized occupation' (US Department of Education 2014b). In her 2015 article for London's *Financial Times,* Gillian Tett sharply captured the problem in recording the views of Sarah Bloom Raskin, the US Deputy Treasury Secretary: 'it is hard for anyone to monitor what is going on because student loans have an ecosystem that is as fragmented as the subprime world. Most notably, those $1.3tn loans are being offered, monitored and serviced by numerous different providers' (Tett 2015). Raskin also noted that the rise in student debt had been exacerbated by the long-term stagnation in household incomes over a number of years.

The US Department of Education adopted the gainful employment rule in 2014 as it noted that for-profit institutions providing some 1,400 programmes for around 840,000 students would not pass its accountability standards. Students graduating

TABLE 2.2 Number of certificates below degree level conferred to US citizens and nonresident aliens, 1998–2014

Year	Total	White	Black	Hispanic	Asian/Pacific Islander	American Indian/ Alaska Native	Two or more races	Non-resi- dent alien
1998–99	555,883	345,359	92,800	76,833	27,920	7,510	–	5,461
1999–2000	558,129	337,546	97,329	81,132	29,361	6,966	–	5,795
2000–01	552,503	333,478	99,397	78,528	28,123	6,598	–	6,379
2001–02	584,248	352,559	106,647	83,950	27,490	7,430	–	6,172
2002–03	646,425	382,289	120,582	95,499	32,981	8,117	–	6,957
2003–04	687,787	402,989	129,891	107,216	32,819	8,375	–	6,497
2004–05	710,873	415,670	133,601	114,089	32,783	8,150	–	6,580
2005–06	715,401	412,077	135,460	118,853	34,110	8,400	–	6,501
2006–07	729,037	420,585	139,995	119,501	32,962	8,793	–	7,201
2007–08	749,883	430,187	145,181	122,676	35,985	8,596	–	7,258
2008–09	804,620	450,562	161,487	138,301	37,941	9,485	–	6,844
2009–10	935,719	511,186	191,657	172,015	41,407	12,003	–	7,451
2010–11	1,030,347	557,595	207,693	187,433	44,294	11,204	14,999	7,259
2011–12	989,061	535,621	190,253	187,014	43,048	10,638	14,140	8,347
2012–13	967,214	524,000	177,006	186,248	44,196	10,824	17,642	7,298
2013–14	969,353	523,184	177,881	185,588	43,810	10,817	19,931	8,142

Source: Author's own drawn from US Department of Education (2014a) National Center for Education Statistics, Integrated Postsecondary Education Data System (IPEDS), Completions survey (IPEDS-C:99); and IPEDS Fall 2000 through Fall 2014.

from such institutions typically moved into low-skilled and low-paid jobs and were unlikely to be able to pay off their student loans:

> The situation for students at for-profit institutions is particularly troubling. On average, attending a two-year for-profit institution costs a student four times as much as attending a community college. More than 80 percent of students at for-profits borrow, while less than half of students at public institutions do. Ultimately, students at for-profit colleges represent only about 11 percent of the total higher education population but 44 percent of all federal student loan defaults.
>
> *US Department of Education (2014b)*

A two-year study for the US Senate on the US for-profit college sector reported that

> Publicly traded companies operating for-profit colleges had an average profit margin of 19.7 percent, generated a total of $3.2 billion in pre-tax profit and paid an average of $7.3 million to their chief executive officers in 2009 … In 2009–10, the sector received $32 billion, 25 percent of the total Department of Education student aid program funds … rising from $1.1 billion in the 2000–1 school year to $7.5 billion in the 2009–10 school year.
>
> *United States Senate Health, Education, Labor and Pensions Committee (2012)*

The devolved and poorly regulated provision of vocational education in the USA has created significant opportunities for private enterprise to capture parts of the federal and state-created market, especially in the provision of shorter courses, often for those from socially disadvantaged backgrounds. Many provide credentials of little benefit to the students who take them. By 2010, state aid, via student loans, to the for-profit sector represented about 80 per cent of its income, with a significant proportion of graduates falling into the subprime category of being unable to pay off the loans incurred during the course of their studies. The emergence of the subprime student, however, has not only arisen in vocational education.

Higher education

Anxiety about national economic performance has not been confined to vocational education; universities too have been drawn toward instrumentalism. Universities have been increasingly concerned to demonstrate their contribution to the economic performance of their local and national economies.[7] Higher education reform has been wrapped in the language of widening access and improving educational opportunity for those from socially disadvantaged backgrounds. The expansion and increasing diversity of provision has given rise to major debates about funding. The cost problem has been addressed by a significant change in funding arrangements, with state-supported loan systems underpinning the shift toward households, rather than general taxation, absorbing an increasing share of the current and future costs

TABLE 2.3 Students obtaining first degree, UK and USA, 1960–2012

	UK	USA
1960	22,426	365,174
1970	51,189	839,730
1980	68,150	935,140
1990	77,163	1,094,358
2000	243,246	1,244,171
2012	350,800	1,716,053

Sources: Author's own drawn from US National Center for Education Statistics and Bolton, P. (2012) Education: historical statistics standard note: SN/SG/4252 House of Commons Library, November 2012.

of university education. These developments have tended to undermine the very concept of the public university and have been reflected in the employment status of staff. In the UK, for example, universities are now classified as being outside of the public sector and designated as Non-Profit Institutions Serving Households (NPISH). The last two of these features are discussed below in a little more detail.

The funding of higher education in the USA and UK exemplifies the state's role in moving from the containment of the costs of its massification (Table 2.3) in the last decades of the twentieth century to the financializing of its consumption in the new century. The designation in the UK of the sector's role as 'serving households' is not merely a matter of statistical reclassification, it is rather indicative of how the financing of higher education now relies upon increasingly unstable debt-based foundations. In the UK, government support has four dimensions: teaching grants, research grants, student maintenance grants and student loans. The teaching grant was cut by over 40 per cent between 2010–11 and 2014–15 from just over £7 billion to £4 billion, research funding by 7 per cent, and in 2016 the government announced that from 2016–17 maintenance grants would be replaced by loans.

In the USA, many of the Ivy League universities are private not-for-profit institutions while public universities are funded by their states, typically constituting the third largest item of expenditure in their budgets. Over recent years the funding per full-time equivalent student (FTE) has declined as state budgets have been squeezed. State funding is focused on operational support for institutions while federal spending is mainly for financial assistance to students, federal research projects, and veterans' education benefits (American Academy of Arts and Sciences 2015).

In the USA over the period 2006 to 2015, student debt levels rose from $481 billion to about $1.3 trillion; in England over the same period students' publicly owned debt rose from £14 billion to a little under £65 billion (Figures 2.1 and 2.2). The UK's Office for Budget Responsibility's estimate of the impact of the reforms on the student loan system (undertaken prior to more recent announcements on maintenance grants becoming loans and the removal of the cap in numbers universities may accept in each year) indicated that '[t]he (cumulative) addition to debt increases rapidly from 3.4 per cent of GDP before peaking at almost 10 per cent

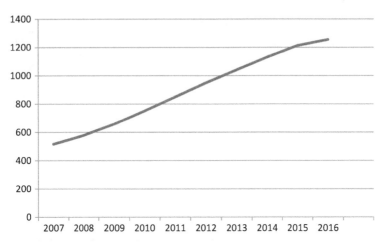

FIGURE 2.1 Federal student aid portfolio summary, 2007–2016 (dollars outstanding in billions)
Source: Author's own from Federal Student Aid (2016) National Student Loan Data System (NSLDS) for Students, Federal Student Aid.

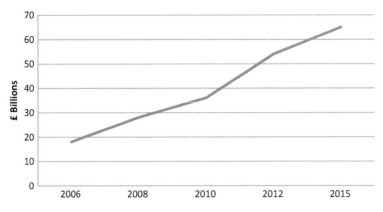

FIGURE 2.2 UK student loans; amount of public debt outstanding
Source: Author's own from Bolton, P. (2016b) *Briefing Paper Number 1079: Student Loan Statistics*, London: House of Commons, 20 January 2016

in the mid-2030s. This would be equivalent to around £450 billion in 2013–14 prices' (Bolton 2016b:16).

Whilst the student debt problem has been widely debated in the USA and compared to the subprime mortgage issues that triggered the 2007–8 financial crisis, the level of debt arising from student loans is considerably lower than that which triggered the last major financial crisis. The rise in the debt burden has, however, generated a state-induced market in higher education that mirrors that of the vocational education sector. The rapid growth of for-profit colleges and universities has been facilitated by their adoption of many of the characteristics of

McDonaldization[8] – on-line learning, extensive and aggressive approaches to recruitment and the use of part-time faculty, through which labour costs have been kept relatively low. The indirect state support for for-profit institutions is illustrated by the Apollo Education Group (owners of the University of Phoenix).

In 2015 the University of Phoenix, operated across several states in the USA, had net revenue of $2.5 billion, 84 per cent of which was derived from federal grant aid. It employed 23,000 faculty (about 1800 of which were full-time) and 11,000 non-faculty. Of the top 20 schools owed most arising from student debt, 13 were for-profit schools in 2014 (up from just one for-profit school in 2001). Of these, three were in the top four – the University of Phoenix's students owed $35.5 billion, Walden University $8.9 billion and DeVry University $8.2 billion.

Apollo Education, founded in the mid-1970s, went public in 1994. Its rapid expansion in the early years of this century (through the growth in student numbers at the University of Phoenix) ensured its stock market value rose significantly during the period of the financial crisis, reaching a high in 2009 of $78 dollars per share. Since that high point its performance has waned as the federal government and a wider public became increasingly aware of the for-profit sector's aggressive approach to student recruitment, particularly focused on lower-income students and their poor completion and employment records. Apollo and many other companies' revenue relied almost exclusively on the federal loans provided to students. In the last two years, Apollo Education and other colleges have witnessed declining enrolment arising from adverse publicity, a series of high-profile lawsuits and tighter government regulation. By early 2016, it appeared that Apollo Education would be purchased by several private equity firms, its future resting, in part, upon its overseas expansion via the acquisition of such companies as BPP, one of the few private institutions that have achieved the designation of university status in the UK.

Perhaps the rapid growth phase of for-profit institutions is coming to a close in the United States, but the private sector's engagement in the education sector is likely to continue and expand through outsourced educational services offered by educational technology companies (including the expansion of Massive Open Online Courses). In short, it seems that the US state may be maker and moderator of a quasi-market in post-compulsory education with the student loan system producing, albeit on a smaller scale, its own form of fictitious capital ($1.3 trillion debt outstanding in 2016), courses of questionable quality and a huge debt problem for those with the least future capacity to pay it off.

As the USA, under the Obama Administration, has tightened its regulation of post-compulsory education, the UK is set in mid-2016 to loosen the regulations affecting the capacity of for-profit institutions to operate in the UK. The Conservative government's productivity plan, published in July 2015, included further reforms to UK's higher education system with its promise to 'open the higher education market to more new entrants to stimulate competition and innovation, increase choice for students, and deliver better value for money' (HM Treasury 2015:9). Arden University, formerly known as Resource Development International, duly secured accreditation as a UK university in summer 2015. Arden is owned by the US-based Capella Education Company and offers specialist distance learning degrees in partnership with established universities such as Bradford, Sunderland and Anglia Ruskin (as well as vocational BTEC qualifications with Pearson, former owners of the *Financial Times*). Arden was accredited by the Department for Business, Innovation and Skills rather than by the traditional and longer route of Privy Council approval, taking its place alongside three other for-profit universities operating in the UK: BPP University, the University of Law and Regent's University London.

Though for-profit universities constitute a small proportion of the UK's system, it seems likely that the Conservative government's reforms will create opportunities for their expansion. While the UK has retained a tighter regulatory control over the sector than the US, similar trends have emerged in the form of student loans generating a significant rise – over £60 billion by the end of 2015 – in outstanding public debt (Figure 2.2).

The future of this 'market' in the UK rests upon the capacity of the state to manage the rapidly rising debt level through, for example, selling the student loan book to the private sector, ensuring a higher percentage of debt recovery than achieved hitherto or by capping student fee levels. Continued capping of fee levels is the opposite of the Conservative government's intentions as set out in its productivity plan. Improving the level of debt recovery (either by selling to the private sector or by increased efforts by government agencies) rests upon broader improvements in the earnings of graduates and in the capacity of the economy to create better paid graduate jobs.[9]

Conclusion

The shift to 'household' funding in both the UK and USA has created what some commentators have called a 'state-induced' market or, more accurately, a competitive framework for the recruitment of students in vocational and higher education. This framework is underpinned by a significant rise over the past decade in the current and projected public debt levels required to support the student loan systems that, in turn, have created a new generation of graduates – subprime students – saddled with debts that their future earnings are unlikely to enable them to meet. This funding approach is deeply flawed given the level of public debt outstanding in 2016 and its projected growth in future decades. It parodies the role of the credit-based patterns of consumption that characterize the wider, highly financialized US and British economies.

The increasing engagement by the state of the private sector in educational provision has arisen in part from the attempts by the former to contain costs. In turn, private enterprise has entered the sector seeking solid rates of return, the funding of which is increasingly underwritten by public debt. Many of these enterprises may be characterized as state dependent for their revenues. Often drawn into the sector by the reduced risk associated with state-backed student loans, some private-sector enterprises have flourished whilst others have folded. The most successful now operate across the UK, USA and other areas of the world and seek to develop specific niches, not least in providing training and education to socially deprived communities whose young people often have little choice but to become 'subprime' students.

Over the course of the long depression, successive UK and American governments have associated education reform with reference to an instrumentalist narrative. The ideological hold of vocationalism has strengthened as the economies of both nations have continued to stagnate. This instrumentalism has damagingly limited education's social and public purpose but has also served to legitimize the financialization of its funding. Widespread acceptance of education as an asset that accrues to the individual provides an ideological prop to the shifting of its cost to those who are its supposed beneficiaries. The funding of vocational and higher education in the UK and the USA rests on thin ice. The increasing diversity of providers cannot disguise their rising financial dependence upon student loan systems underwritten by a growing public debt. Deferring debt, even that underwritten by the state, means that significant parts of the education sector in the USA and the UK are living on borrowed time.

Notes

1 The long depression refers here to the protracted period of low- and no-growth experienced by Western economies since the early 1970s. This lack of productive dynamism is historically unprecedented in its duration.
2 See Marginson, S. (1993) *Education and Public Policy in Australia*. Cambridge: Cambridge University Press.
3 There are several studies of the instrumental and cultural 'turns' in education policy and practice in Britain and the USA during this period. For sharply argued and more detailed analysis than can be explored in this text see, for example, Brown, P. (2006) The Opportunity Trap, in Lauder, H., Brown P., Dillabough, J. and Halsey A.H. (eds.) *Education, Globalisation and Social Change*, Oxford: OUP: 381–97; Tomlinson, S. (2011) *Education in a Post-Welfare Society*, Maidenhead: Open University Press; and Ecclestone, K. and Hayes, D. (2009) *The Dangerous Rise of Therapeutic Education*, Abingdon: Routledge.
4 An extensive literature on this shift has been written. For example, Hyland examined the reductionist trend in the UK's vocational and educational training (VET) over this period: Amongst this 'flurry of reforms' were the many schemes associated with the 'new vocationalism' (Avis *et al.* 1996; Ainley 1999) of the 1980s and 1990s such as the various Youth Training Schemes (YTS) designed to remedy the deficiencies of school-leavers by supplying them with employability skills, Training Credits, and the introduction of competence-based education and training (CBET) through National Vocational Qualifications (NVQs). None of these came close to solving the perennial problems of VET and some of them – in particular YTS and the emergence of 'skilltalk' that CBET popularised through NVQs – have, arguably, managed to aggravate matters by impoverishing the epistemological and general theoretical foundation of vocational pursuits, thereby devaluing training at all levels. See Hyland, T. (2006) Reductionist Trends in Education and Training for Work: Skills, Competences and Work-based Learning, *Education Conference Paper 2*: http://digitalcommons.bolton.ac.uk,ed.conference2.
5 See Gibbons, S., Machin, S. and Silva, O. (2006) The Educational Impact of Parental Choice and School Competition, *Centre Piece* Winter 2006/07: http://cep.lse.ac.uk/pubs/download/CP216.pdf.
6 Education is third after health and defence for PFI projects in the UK (£7.7 billion of capital cost and £29 billion of future PFI repayments). Interest rates on government

repayments rose significantly in the wake of the 2007–8 financial crash, prompting widespread criticism of PFI as a live-now-pay-later scheme. See Commons Select Committee (2011) Committee publishes report on private finance initiative funding, 19 August: http://www.parliament.uk/business/committees/committees-az/commons-select/treasury-committee/news/pfi-report/.

7 Several universities have estimated their impacts upon their local economies. For example, in a 2016 report produced by Oxford Economics, the University of Bath estimated that it provided 6.25 per cent of total economic output of its region (http://www.bath.ac.uk/news/2016/02/12/uni-contributes-294m-to-local-economy/), and the combined contributions of Leeds University and Leeds Beckett University to the local economy is estimated to be just under £1.7 billion (http://www.leedsbeckett.ac.uk/about-our-university/facts-and-figures/; https://www.leeds.ac.uk/info/5000/about/140/facts_and_figures). While a proportion of such totals arise from entrepreneurial activity, much is derived from the redistributive effects of direct and indirect state funding (student loans). In effect, higher education institutions have become very important components of local economies, often helping compensate for the long-term impact of de-industrialisation on the towns and cities in which they are located.

8 Low-cost, standardized modes of education delivery are characteristics of McDonaldization. See Ritzer, G. (1998) *The McDonaldization Thesis,* pp. 151–62, and Hayes, D. and Wynyard, R. (eds.) (2002) *The McDonaldization of Higher Education.*

9 Recent influential reports have questioned assumptions about the virtues of continuing to expand the numbers in HE and the basis of the funding of its expansion. A report for the CIPD by Craig Holmes and Ken Mayhew (2015) *Over-qualification and Skills Mismatch in the Graduate Labour Market,* concluded, for example, that 'Our findings suggest that the presence of a large HE sector will not necessarily lead to the attainment of the knowledge economy so beloved by successive UK governments' (http://www.cipd.co.uk/binaries/over-qualification-and-skills-mismatch-graduate-labour-market.pdf). This view broadly supports those of Alison Wolf. See Wolf, A. (2015) *Issues and Ideas: Heading for the Precipice: Can Further and Higher Education Funding Policies be Sustained?* The Policy Institute at King's College London.

References

Ainley, P. (1999) *Learning Policy: Towards the Certified Society,* London: Palgrave Macmillan.

American Academy of Arts and Sciences (2015) Public Research Universities: Changes in State Funding: https://www.amacad.org/multimedia/pdfs/publications/researchpapersmonographs/PublicResearchUniv_ChangesInStateFunding.pdf (accessed 4 May 2016).

Avis, J., Bloomer, M., Esland, G., Gleeson, E. and Hodkinson, P. (1996) *Knowledge and Nationhood: Education, Politics and Work,* London: Cassell.

Babcock (2016) Partners in Education: http://www.babcock-education.co.uk/local-authority-partnerships (accessed 20 May 2016).

Bacon, R. and Eltis, W. (1976) *Britain's Economic Problem: Too Few Producers,* London: MacMillan.

Bailey, T. (1993) The Missions of the TECs and Private Sector Involvement in Training: Lessons from Private Industry Councils, *Oxford Studies in Comparative Education,* 3(1): 7–26.

Ball, S. (2007) *Education plc: Understanding Private Sector Participation in Education,* London: Routledge.

Bolton, P. (2012) Education: Historical Statistics Standard Note: SN/SG/4252, House of Commons Library, November 2012: http://researchbriefings.files.parliament.uk/documents/SN04252/SN04252.pdf (accessed 16 March 2016).

Bolton, P. (2016a) *Briefing Paper Number 1079: Student Loan Statistics,* London: House of Commons, 20 January 2016.

Bolton, P. (2016b) HE in England from 2012: Funding and Finance, London: House of Commons Briefing Paper Number 6206, 29 January 2016.

Brenner, R. (2002) *The Boom and the Bubble: The US in the World Economy*, London: Verso.

Brown, P. (2006) The Opportunity Trap, in Lauder, H., Brown, P., Dillabough, J. and Halsey, A. H. (eds.) *Education, Globalisation and Social Change*, Oxford: Oxford University Press.

Bullock, P. and Yaffe, D. (1974) Inflation, The Crisis and the Post War Boom, *Revolutionary Communist Number 3/4*, London: RCG Publications Ltd.

Castells, M. (2001) *The Internet Galaxy*, Oxford: Oxford University Press.

Catalyst Corporate Finance (2014) Education and Training M & A update: http://www.catalystcf.co.uk/research-documents/2014/16-education-and-training-sector-report-spring-2014.pdf (accessed 12 May 2016).

Clarke, S. (1994) *Marx's Theory of Crisis*, London: MacMillan.

Collaborative Academies Trust (2015) Annual Report and Financial Statements 2014–2015: http://collaborativeacademiestrust.org/wordpress/wp-content/uploads/2016/01/8168307-Collaborative-Academies-Trust-1415-FinStat2.pdf (accessed 18 May 2016).

Commons Select Committee (2011) Committee Publishes Report on Private Finance Initiative Funding, 19 August: http://www.parliament.uk/business/committees/committees-a-z/commons-select/treasury-committee/news/pfi-report/ (accessed 16 March 2016).

Department of Education and Science (1977) Education in Schools: A Consultative Document, London: Her Majesty's Stationery Office: http://www.educationengland.org.uk/documents/des1977/educinschools.html (accessed 16 March 2016).

Dixon, H. (2014) Academies Paying Millions to Businesses Linked to Their Directors, *Telegraph*, 13 January: http://www.telegraph.co.uk/education/educationnews/10567498/Academies-paying-millions-to-businesses-linked-to-their-directors.html (accessed 18 May 2016).

Ecclestone, K. and Hayes, D. (2009) *The Dangerous Rise of Therapeutic Education*, Abingdon: Routledge.

Engdahl, F. (2006) Crisis of the US Dollar System, *Global Research*, 14 October: http://www.globalresearch.ca/crisis-of-the-u-s-dollar-system/3482 (accessed 2 April 2016).

Federal Student Aid (2016) National Student Loan Data System (NSLDS) for Students, Federal Student Aid: https://www.nslds.ed.gov/nslds/nslds_SA/ (accessed 16 March 2016).

Finegold, D., McPharland, L. and Richardson, W. (1993) *Something Borrowed, Something Learned?: The Transatlantic Market in Education and Training Reform*, Washington: Brookings Institute Press.

Gamble, A. (2009) *The Spectre at the Feast*, Basingstoke: Palgrave MacMillan.

Gibbons, S., Machin, S. and Silva, O. (2006) The Educational Impact of Parental Choice and School Competition, *Centre Piece Winter 2006/07*: http://cep.lse.ac.uk/pubs/download/CP216.pdf (accessed 16 March 2016).

Glyn, A. (2006) *Capitalism Unleashed*, Oxford: Oxford University Press.

Gordon, R. J. (2016) *The Rise and Fall of American Growth: The U.S. Standard of Living since the Civil War*, Princeton: Princeton University Press.

Hall, P. (2000) *Cities in Civilization*, London: Phoenix.

Harvey, D. (2007) *A Brief History of Neo-Liberalism*, Oxford: Oxford University Press.

Hayes, D. and Wynyard, R. (eds.) (2002) *The McDonaldization of Higher Education*, Westport, CT, and London: Bergin and Garvey.

HM Treasury (2015) Fixing the Foundations: Creating a More Prosperous Nation: https://www.gov.uk/government/uploads/system/uploads/attachment_data/file/443898/Productivity_Plan_web.pdf (accessed 3 April 2016).

Hodgson, A. (ed.) (2015) *The Coming of Age for FE?: Reflections on the Past and Future Role of Further Education Colleges in England*, London: Institute of Education Press.

Holmes, C. and Mayhew, K. (2015) Over-qualification and Skills Mismatch in the Graduate Labour Market, CIPD Policy Report, London, 18 August: http://www.cipd.co.uk/bina ries/over-qualification-and-skills-mismatch-graduate-labour-market.pdf (accessed 15 March 2016).

Hyland, T. (2006) Reductionist Trends in Education and Training for Work: Skills, Competences and Work-Based Learning, Education Conference Paper 2: http://digitalcommons. bolton.ac.uk,ed.conference2 (accessed 16 March 2016).

Kliman, A. (2014) *The Failure of Capitalist Production*, London: Pluto Press.

Lapavitsas, C. (2013) *Profiting without Producing*, London: Verso.

Marginson, S. (1993) *Education and Public Policy in Australia*, Cambridge: Cambridge University Press.

Mattick, P. (2011) *Business as Usual*, London: Reaktion Books Ltd.

Minsky, H. (1986) *Stabilising an Unstable Economy*, New Haven: Yale University Press.

Mokyr, J. (2013) Joel Mokyr on Growth, Innovation, and Stagnation, EconTalk episode with Joel Mokyr: http://www.econtalk.org/archives/2013/11/joel_mokyr_on_g.html (accessed 10 March 2016).

National Audit Office (NAO) (2015) Overseeing Financial Sustainability in the Further Education Sector: https://www.nao.org.uk/wp-content/uploads/2015/07/Overseeing-financial-sustainability-in-the-further-education-sector.pdf (accessed 14 March 2016).

OECD (2013) The Global Challenge of Skills – 37 OECD Reviews of Vocational Education and Training: A Skills Beyond School Review of the United States: http://www. oecd.org/employment/ASkillsbeyondSchoolReviewoftheUnitedStates.pdf (accessed 17 April 2016).

Poynter, G. (2012) The Global Recession, in Poynter, G., MacRury, I. and Calcutt, A. (eds.) *London after Recession*, Farnham: Ashgate.

Ritzer, G. (1998) *The McDonaldization Thesis*, Thousand Oaks, CA, and London: Sage Publications.

Susskind, R. E., and Susskind, D. (2015) *The Future of the Professions: How Technology Will Transform the Work of Human Experts*, Oxford: Oxford University Press.

Tett, G. (2015) Debt Hangover Ruins the American Dream, *Financial Times*, 7 May: http:// www.ft.com/cms/s/2/a194e654-f3e1-11e4-a9f3-00144feab7de.html#axzz4Cs5EHWNV (accessed 10 June 2016).

Tomlinson, S. (2011) *Education in a Post-Welfare Society*, Maidenhead: Open University Press.

Trade Union Congress (TUC) (2014) *Education Not for Sale*, London: TUC.

US Department of Education (2013) Characteristics of Public and Private Elementary and Secondary School Teachers in the United States: Results: http://nces.ed.gov/pubs2013/ 2013314.pdf (accessed 17 March 2016).

US Department of Education (2014a) Integrated Postsecondary Education Data System (IPEDS), Completions survey (IPEDS-C: 99); and IPEDS Fall 2000 through Fall 2014, *National Center for Education Statistics*: https://nces.ed.gov/programs/digest/mobile/ SourceInfo.aspx (accessed 16 March 2016).

US Department of Education (2014b) Obama Administration Announces Final Rules to Protect Students from Poor-Performing Career College Programs, October 2014: http:// www.ed.gov/news/press-releases/obama-administration-announces-final-rules-protect-students-poor-performing-career-college-programs (accessed 17 March 2016).

United States Senate Health, Education, Labor and Pensions Committee (2012) For Profit Higher Education: The Failure to Safeguard the Federal Investment and Ensure Student Success, Majority Committee Staff Report and Accompanying Minority Committee Staff

Views, 30 July: http://www.help.senate.gov/imo/media/for_profit_report/PartI-PartIII-SelectedAppendixes.pdf (accessed 14 March 2016).

Whittaker, F. (2015) School Supply Teacher Spending Rockets by 27 Per Cent in Two Years, *Schools Week*, 29 June 2015: http://schoolsweek.co.uk/school-supply-teacher-spending-rockets-by-27-per-cent-in-two-years/ (accessed 20 March 2016).

Wilson, H. (1963) Labour's Plan for Science: http://nottspolitics.org/wp-content/uploads/2013/06/Labours-Plan-for-science.pdf (accessed 2 April 2016).

Wolf, A. (2015) *Issues and Ideas: Heading for the Precipice: Can Further and Higher Education Funding Policies be Sustained?* The Policy Institute at King's College London, June 2015.

3

BEYOND MCDONALDIZATION

A conversation

Dennis Hayes and George Ritzer

George Ritzer and I have had several formal and informal conversations about his powerful contemporary characterisation of Weberian rationalisation through the analogy with McDonald's fast-food restaurants – what he labelled 'McDonaldization'. The first of these discussions was during the conference held at Canterbury Christ Church University on 7 July 2001 (see Panton 2001) that led to the publication of *The McDonaldization of Higher Education* (Hayes and Wynyard 2002) and secondly, and more formally, at another conference at Oxford Brookes University on 13 June 2008 (see Hayes 2008), when we addressed the questions that dominate this book – what will come after McDonaldization if this isn't an ineluctable reality? These and other communications are ephemeral, and with George's agreement we discussed many of them once again in the summer of 2016 to make them available to those who did not hear the original discussions at the conferences or over dinner. Many of the ideas that came out of these conversations were further discussed over almost a decade of discussing McDonaldization with senior Chinese academics on the Leadership Programmes for China in the Department of Continuing Education at the University of Oxford. Some of these ideas went down well, particularly a comment of George that he was 'more of a Weberian pessimist than a Marxist optimist'.

George has given interviews before, and those interested in his personal education and his wider sociological thinking might like to read 'Being (George Ritzer) and nothingness: An interview' (Dandaneau and Dodsworth 2006). It is very instructive about the world of academic publishing, on which perhaps more academics' personal experiences could usefully be shared.

The various conversations usually started with a brief biography of George, so here is one adapted from the University of Maryland website:

> George Ritzer is Distinguished University Professor at the University of Maryland. He has named at Distinguished-Scholar Teacher at Maryland and

received the American Sociological Association's Distinguished Contribution to Teaching Award. In the application of social theory to the social world, his many books include *The McDonaldization of Society* (Eighth Edition 2015), *Enchanting a Disenchanted World* (Third Edition 2010) and *The Globalization of Nothing* (Second Edition 2007). He also edited the eleven-volume *Encyclopedia of Sociology* (2007). His books have been translated into over twenty languages, with over a dozen translations of *The McDonaldization of Society* alone. Referring to the global success of his writings, my colleague Robin Wynyard has described George as 'the living embodiment of the concept of McDonaldization'. Readers can find out more on George's personal website: http://www. georgeritzer.com.

On being George Ritzer

DH: I wonder if you could say what it is like to be George Ritzer? Your academic history is tied up with the concept of McDonaldization. Robin Wynyard, as you know, has described you as 'the living embodiment of the concept'.

GR: What's it like to be George Ritzer? Most people would find it pretty boring – lots of time with books, thoughts and writing and rewriting texts (for example, I will soon begin the 9th edition of *The McDonaldization of Society*, and I am working now on the 4th edition of my *Introduction to Sociology* text). The exciting times for me are when I get new ideas and I am able to flesh them out and expand upon them. Even more exciting are the times when one idea leads to a new one and that, in turn, gets expanded and developed. For example, a brief aside in early editions of *The McDonaldization of Society* on how fast food restaurants put customers to work led to a series of about six to eight papers over the last decade on prosumption. Also exciting is to see what others do with ideas like McDonaldization and more recently with prosumption.

On McDonaldization

DH: Could you explain why the McDonaldization thesis has such a resonance with people? 'Starbuckization' doesn't capture the imagination in the same way.

GR: The McDonaldization thesis is quite clear. The success of the concept is related to McDonald's success. It has been thought to be in decline several times, but roars back every time. It remains an almost universally recognized brand and logo – still better known than Donald Trump! Starbucks has grown in recognition – it is even opening in Italy – but it is not likely to rival McDonald's any time soon.

DH: Has your understanding of McDonaldization changed over time?

GR: I think it remains largely the same. There have been lots of criticisms and lots of alternatives suggested (beyond Starbuckization there's eBayization, etc.), but none have really caused me to change my thinking. The continued popularity of the term and of the book (going into its ninth edition) indicates that most people are quite comfortable with the concept and continue to find it useful.

DH: When we talked in Oxford about the inevitability of McDonaldization and how your writings implied – apart from rare moments of optimism, for example, when you recently introduced the concept of the productive consumer, the prosuming self. I remember you saying in Oxford that you were 'more of a Weberian pessimist than a Marxist optimist'.

GR: That remains the case. While I often use Marxian ideas, I still end up with Weberian pessimism.

DH: How does the thesis apply to the university, to what you have called the McUniversity?

GR: I think I've dealt with this question years ago in my essay on McUniversity. If anything, McUniversity is more ubiquitous than ever, especially in the UK. The rise of online universities, MOOCs [Massive Open Online Courses], and their characteristics make McDonaldization even clearer.

DH: When we first discussed the McDonaldization thesis in Canterbury in 2001 you were surprised how bureaucratic the UK higher education system was. Last year the government announced a new league table, the Teaching Excellence Framework (TEF), to further bureaucratise the university by producing league tables of the best universities for teaching, as they do for research through the Research Excellence Framework (REF). Are universities freer and less McDonaldized in the US?

GR: Yes, that continues to be the case even though American universities have become increasingly McDonaldized. However, the centralized control of universities in the UK makes for a much higher level of McDonaldization. American universities are saved to some degree by their decentralization.

DH: In line with the themes of this book, and your desire, expressed in your chapter in *The McDonaldization of Higher Education*, to 're-enchant' the university, what broad visions of higher education have you to offer as a steer for our thinking today?

GR: Tough one. Always easier to critically analyse than to suggest viable solutions. Further, I really am a Weberian pessimist, and Weber was better at analysis and critique than he was at presenting a new vision. Marx was good on such a vision, but we know where that got us. I don't see happy endings.

Safe spaces

DH: Weber's 'Iron Cage' metaphor doesn't seem to fit – the university as a safe space is comfortable rather than containing.

GR: Sure, safe and comfortable (predictability is one of the dimensions of McDonaldization and it makes the setting safe and comfortable), at least comparatively, but that doesn't mean it's not a cage. It may not feel like an iron cage to most of the 'inmates'; it may be more like one of the other metaphors I used, a 'velvet cage', but it's still a cage. People are less likely to balk, to rebel against a velvet (or 'rubber') cage than one that is made of, and feels like, steel. In a sense, a velvet cage is less likely to put people off, more likely to survive and succeed than one that has the look and feel of steel.

DH: There have been many debates in the US and UK recently about universities needing to be 'safe spaces'. How does this new development fit within the McDonaldization thesis?

GR: On the surface one would think it would make them less McDonaldized, but anything can be McDonaldized. What constitutes a safe space can be McDonaldized, as can the nature of the spaces themselves. We're back to Weber's iron cage – there is no escape.

DH: Students are demanding safe spaces. Is this the ultimate desire for customer satisfaction at McUniversity? No more experimenting with ideas (although it took them a long time – even McDonald's introduced the Egg McMuffin)?

GR: All cages are 'safe', but that doesn't make them less cagelike. Even if that satisfies students, it isn't necessarily good for them from an intellectual point of view.

On global de-McDonaldization

DH: You said in the 2002 book that the four features of the McUniversity need to be reversed: it must become inefficient, unpredictable, incalculable and uncontrolled. Has this potential for reversal vanished? Must we give up on the university?

GR: I'm a Weberian pessimist on such issues, and I never saw much chance of reversing the process of McDonaldization – of de-McDonaldization – in the university, or anywhere else. Limited efforts can work here or there, but as there are more universities, students, professors, etc., there will be more rather than less McDonaldization. I still think we need to fight against McDonaldization to create less or non-McDonaldized alternatives to it in our classrooms and with our students, but with the knowledge that our successes will be limited.

DH: When you visit China, McDonald's is everywhere – there is the smallest McDonald's in the world at the base of the Pearl Tower in Shanghai. Does the McUniversity meet the educational needs of developing economies? When I challenged some Indian VCs about this they said, bluntly, that for most people the McUniversity was all that was needed, but the elite could have something more exciting and creative. To me this means those countries fear or have given up on human potential.

GR: Sure, a developing country with a huge and growing population like China needs cheap, mass education. This is true, although less so, for most countries – even the US, Great Britain, and so on, but they are much smaller countries and can afford more less-McDonaldized or even non-McDonaldized universities. The elites everywhere will be able to get a high quality, non-McDonaldized education, but such an education will even be more unlikely in the future than it is today for the vast majority of the population.

But maybe the solution lies in the prosumer of education and the advanced technologies that allow more and more people to produce their education as they consume it. Non-McDonaldized universities allow students a greater ability to play a more productive role in their education than large McDonaldized universities. However, new and even unforeseen technological developments on the internet and elsewhere may empower the prosuming student to an unprecedented degree, freeing the student from the limits of a bureaucratized and rationalized university structure, even one that is less or even non-McDonaldized. Of course, a global internet makes mass McDonaldization more rather than less likely. McDonald's has co-opted the prosumer in its global operations; what is to prevent the co-optation of the prosuming student?

A final comment: the necessity of a battle of ideas

DH: Students do need to be free 'from the limits of a bureaucratized and rationalized university structure'. But they need to be free intellectually, not because of their role as putative producers and consumers. They need to be convinced intellectually of the potential of humanity. McDonald's restaurants and the McDonaldized university were both attempts to offer a decent meal and a decent academic experience for everyone who went through the Golden Arches or entered the quad. What I have called the Paradox of McDonaldization is an expression of why McDonaldization is destructive although its intention is to do something that will provide a university education for all. The very processes that are introduced to ensure that higher education is available for all undermine higher education (see Hayes, Chapter 1 in this volume).

What will free students is not any institutional development or process. They have to be part of a cultural battle of ideas about why the university is more than a safe space. Then they can make a choice and either make a difference to the university by making it an intellectual 'unsafe space' or choosing to live in a therapeutic 'velvet cage'. Freedom requires the freedom to choose not to be free, but few students will make that choice. Let the battle begin.

References

Dandaneau, S. P. and Dodsworth, R. M. (2006) Being (George Ritzer) and nothingness: An interview, *The American Sociologist*, December 2006, 3(4): 84–96.
Hayes, D. (2008) After McDonaldization – food for thought, *Teaching News*, Oxford Brookes University, Summer 2008: https://wiki.brookes.ac.uk/display/teachingnews/After+McDonaldization+-+food+for+thought (accessed 19 August 2016).
Hayes, D. and Wynyard, R. (eds.) (2002) *The McDonaldization of Higher Education*, Westport, CT: Bergin and Garvey.
Panton, J. (2001) McEducation and bits on the side, spiked, 18 July: http://www.spiked-online.com/newsite/article/11410#.V7xmGpgrLIU (accessed 19 August 2016).

4

BEYOND MCUNIVERSITY

The university as it should be

Angus Kennedy

The university was an ideal of how society should be. The university we have is a sad reflection of what society has become. The university we need will have to be built anew from the ground up.

The university, as Plato founded it, and as we knew it in the post-Reformation Age of Enlightenment, was itself a society, a self-selecting congregation of scholars, dedicated to the pursuit of truth. The project was sacred and alchemic: the turning of facts into theories which explained them, the turning of the many into the one. Academics turned away from the confusing multiplicity of the real to the ivory tower promise of unifying ideals. The very word, 'university', in Latin *universitas*, means what results after a-turning-into-one – it is the unity created by diverse individuals from discordant realities, it is the whole, the *totum*, the universe, the world. It is both the whole world that humanistic universalism reveals and creates, and it is the society that espouses that universalism: the scholastic community united in its pursuit of truth, dedicated to following the light of its reasoned inquiry, *wherever* it might lead it.

The university, if we trace its logico-historical development, was founded on the basis of the freedom of its members to pursue the truth without obstruction. For Plato that meant a withdrawal from the all-too-real dangers of involvement in politics, a withdrawal to the edge of the city, to the groves of Academe, and a barring of entry to those not of a like mind (or, seen the other way, the creation of a community of the like-minded): let no one ignorant of geometry enter here, so said the sign over the door to the Academy. Why geometry? Because God was the divine geometer. The scholar was doing God's work in studying the mathematical truths that underpinned and made sense of this ever-changing and unstable material world. The form of the Good for Plato was a beautiful unity not to be found in this world of shadows but an ideal that his fellow Academics could hope to see with the light of the mind, on a quest to bring back that knowledge to the rest of mankind languishing in the cave of the real. The university was not a few marginal eccentrics on the fringes of society; it was the means by which society itself was to be liberated from the bonds of ignorance, materialism, greed, and conflict.

The first universities of the Middle Ages, Bologna, Paris, and Oxford, were seats of religious instruction, debate, and research – the evolution of cathedral and monastery schools – concerned with questions of heresy and the need to establish the truth. They were urban and urbane both: teaching the seven liberal arts of arithmetic, geometry, astronomy, and music (the *quadrivium*), and the core subjects of grammar, logic, and rhetoric (the *trivium*). These arts were *liberal* because they were the arts worthy of a free individual, a *liber*, someone able to take his place in society, and in the company of others, as an equal. An institution like Bologna was based on the freedom to study the business of being free, and this free pursuit of freedom was a self-conscious project – Bologna was set up as an autonomous degree-awarding body, independent of both Holy Roman Empire and Holy Mother Church. Its charter, the *constitutio habita*, enshrined the academic freedom of the travelling scholar in a right to unhindered passage in the interests of education. The medieval Christian university was also on a journey: to reconcile the phenomena of the natural world, as revealed in the works of Aristotle, with the teachings of the Church about the nature of the truth as revealed in the Bible. Human reason could hope to reconcile the two (Flesh and Word) and explain man's place in the world.

The development of the *humanities* in the Renaissance, hand in hand with the exploration, civilisation, and increasing *humanisation of the world*, gave greater emphasis to grammar and rhetoric and to history, the study of the classics, poetry and moral philosophy. The Reformation too was both a reflection of and a spur to the further emancipation of the individual, free to follow God in his own way. Martin Luther was a Renaissance scholar, studying ancient languages, translating them into the demotic (*Am Anfang schuf Gott Himmel und Erde*) and discarding tradition where it had ossified into prejudice and error. And it was to be German Lutherans in the age of Enlightenment that took the university into the modern world and to its highest point. The famous self-discipline and eccentricity of Immanuel Kant, in his devotion to the life of the mind, epitomised – maybe created – the archetype of the university professor: withdrawn from the world, withdrawn even from the university for ten years in which he thought through the very possibility of our knowledge of the world. Kant's loneliness, or at least the myth of it, speaks to the fundamental importance for society of living on the edge of things. It is only from the edge of the world that we can gain perspective upon it. It is at the edge that we push forward the boundaries of human knowledge. It is at the limit that scholars and academics take point for humanity.

For Kant, at the beginning of the end of the university, like Plato at its beginning, there was something in the structure of the human subject and of the natural object that held out the possibility of knowledge, of achieving unity. Yet Kant's position was that of a radical humanist: for him the free subject came first, determined the object, rather than the other way round. It is precisely because humans have a perspective on the world that there arises the *idea*, the phantom possibility, of a world seen from no point of view at all: a completely objective world. The only thing we can ever be really sure of, however, is that my point of view is *mine*. *My* knowledge of *my* experiences cannot be mistaken about, in the end, at least one thing: that they are *my* experiences. In other words, I come before the world: the unity of my self-consciousness is not something given to me by or through experience of the world; it is instead a presupposition of experience itself. Rather than being a given of experience – a mere fact or datum – I am a creator of what I experience.

With this we are very far from Plato in the sense that he sought to find in *nature*, in the harmonic beauty and form of things, the rules that would show mankind how to live in peace. With Kant, however, we find imperatives for living according to our own *reason,* and the possibility of harmony, even perpetual peace, rests in the *shared reason*, the *common* sense, of all self-conscious beings. But we are still very close to the spirit of the ancient Greeks in their jealous love of freedom which led them to see man as the measure of all things, man as the centre of the universe, and self-knowledge at the heart of that experience.

It was the spirit of both Plato and Kant, however, that lay behind the sweeping reforms of the German university system in the early nineteenth century, reforms that established the foundations of the modern university as we knew it: based on the idea of the scholar as both teacher and researcher; one foot in the camp of the real, the other in the ideal. The concept of *Wissenschaftideologie* was central to these new universities as places concerned, as Friedrich Schleiermacher, the philosopher and liberal theologian, put it, 'with the initiation of a process ... nothing less than a whole new intellectual life process, to awake the idea of learning (*Wissenschaft*) in youth ... so that it becomes second nature for them to consider everything from the point of view of learning' (Watson 2010: 229). This *Wissenschaft* was the knowledge of the unity of the Real and the Ideal – everyone could benefit from becoming educated, through the process of *Bildung* or self-development. Everyone should have the freedom to develop individual creativity, and that creativity, as Wilhelm von Humboldt, the great educational theorist and founder of Berlin University, demanded, should be left alone to lead where it would. Maximum academic freedom would foster a climate in which students grew both into autonomy as individuals but also into *universalists*: citizens of the world. Rejecting what he thought was the over-regulation and restrictive discipline of the French system and of Frederick's Prussian state, von Humboldt liberated students and faculty alike to follow their own path, guided only by the classics of tradition, in particular Ancient Greek language and literature.

The opening up of the university to the creativity innate in everyone meant that universities became much more than just places where knowledge was handed down, generation to generation, but rather places where knowledge was actually created, through independent research and study. While the authority of the classics, let alone of tradition itself, was not yet in question, the new authority of the professor, as a creator of knowledge, was bound to eclipse it in time. Nonetheless, despite the emerging influence and eventual dominance of new *studies,* the liberal humanities remained firmly rooted in the study of the best of the past until the middle of the last century. The importance of the classics, or maybe of the concept of a 'classic', was thought to be central to the ability to judge for oneself, to autonomy in other words. It allowed one to see what was good and what was not and therefore to discriminate between the two. And this ability to be one's own judge of what was best was central to the concept of *Bildung.* One could not expect to develop the best moral character one could if one just followed the rules because they were laid down before one – *as* the rules – by one's betters. The moral impetus had to come from within. So long as society – and its universities – still retained a common sense of what *good* was, understood in terms primarily of its cultural inheritance of literature, art, philosophy, history, the humanities generally and broadly, then one did not need to travel the road to self-understanding entirely on one's own. While maintaining complete freedom to branch off and take new turnings, there was no shame in starting off on well-trodden tracks nor, in fact, in following them all the way with like-minded companions. That is to say, the university could offer its students a grounding in a shared culture widely understood to represent the historic high points of human development and expression but could at the same time allow that some students might reach new heights of their own.

And so, in John Henry Cardinal Newman's famous 1852 lectures on *The Idea of a University*, the university is defined as a community of thinkers committed to intellectual pursuits as ends in themselves. Newman believed not in narrow specialisation but in a broad liberal education that would teach students 'to think and to reason and to compare and to discriminate and to analyse' (Newman 1907: 166). In other words, to judge for themselves. He argued that the ability to judge is developed through exposure to a tradition of the best that has been thought and said; this allows the student to use the great works of the canon as touchstones of truth and beauty against which they can measure what they encounter in the here and now. In this Newman is very much in the age-old spirit of the university: its mission to demonstrate the essential relationship of the ideal and the real in the life-world of the educated and in the educating discipline of truth. Newman is very much in the line of Socrates and Plato too in his insistence that without this ability to judge what was true, students would fall in with whatever was popular at the moment and live in 'happy conformity in ethical character to the age which admires them' (Newman 1907: xxii). His insistence then, on the value of tradition in creating the ability to judge, is precisely to allow students to have the freedom to live non-traditionally if that is what they judge to be best. As Socrates had it, the price of going along with what everyone else thinks was a price not worth paying if it meant living in discord with oneself, if it meant being out of tune with one's own conscience. In moments like that, when the individual fell out with society, the university represented a place of safe distance and tolerance.

Newman, of course, was writing in the defence of the university as offering a broad liberal education because the university of his day was just starting to become ever more specialised. And he was defending its role in defying everyday routine conformity because he saw society as becoming increasingly conformist, bureaucratic, dull, and mechanical. Within 50 years the move in America towards universities becoming research institutions first, and liberal arts colleges second, was already well underway. The real value of Newman is to show us, towards its end, what the university had been. The university was a sacred space founded on the basis of the freedom of its members to pursue the truth. It allowed for disagreement and dispute between those members but within the context of a collegiate and collective life which all shared and to whose overarching discipline they freely submitted. The university was created because society believed certain things to be true and to be good and, as such, to be worth preserving, worth handing on to the next generation. Some things should endure even after the death of the men that had made them; in a way, there should be the possibility of the ideal outliving the real. That preservation and care, and development, of society's ideals, or the ideal of society if you like, was placed in the hands of a special body of men and in a special institution, the university, a place where the values we all shared were to be looked after on our behalf by those best placed to do so. Rather than being in anyway *relevant* to society, instead the role of the university was to be a model of how society should be. Its foundation showed that society believed there were higher things, things more important than the material and mundane, and that they were the rightful objects of study by those who had a higher calling, a more noble profession than soldiery, or buying and selling in the marketplace.

The university has traditionally been sited some distance from major urban centres in order to afford a perspective on society rather than being always in the thick of it. Ideals are always in the distance, on the horizon. When universities and colleges have been built within major cities, they have distanced themselves from it as much as possible, remaining cloistered and separate. The university, if it is to operate as an ideal of how society could be, cannot afford to be too much a part of society as it is. The university, dedicated to the pursuit of truth and to the preservation of the freedom that pursuit requires, is a model of tolerance in that it gives space to people and to ideas that society at large may consider to be useless at best, if not downright subversive. The university can be usefully compared to going on a walk in the middle of the day. The walk is a break with one's work, but it is a break that affords one distance and perspective on that activity. Sometimes insights and new thoughts pop into one's head in the course of the walk. Sometimes nothing happens at all, nothing except, of course, the pleasure and goodness of walking for its own sake.

The university as a model for society showed the possibility of turning the many into the one, of reconciling our individual differences, needs and wants into a harmonious and tolerant social whole through the process of education, both learning and teaching. It reminded us of our better natures and offered us the opportunity to become the best people we could: living free and independent lives of our own determining. It represented too our debt to the next generation, that they should not be denied access to the same cultural inheritance we had enjoyed.

And above all, perhaps, as a sacred space dedicated to universal freedom, it showed us that society is the freely made creation of free individuals who make society possible through the mutual recognition and acknowledgement of each other's freedom.

The university as it is today – at least across most of the Western world – has become a reflection of what society is. The ideal has been subordinated to the imperatives of the real. If higher education retains any purpose beyond mere credentialism, it is only to perform a *function* on behalf of society, supplying it with research that brings scientific advancement and economic advantage, feeding it the trained minds that industry demands, and making sure that its students are happy, *well-adjusted*, model citizens. Far from being an ivory tower – at the limit of the real – the university has succumbed to decades of assault from without (to become more realistic, more relevant to society, more useful) and from within (to sweep away all that stuffy, musty classical elitism and devotion to Truth in favour of a fawning turn to the 'truths' of the excluded Other, the cultures of the post-colonial oppressed, women, and minorities of every kind). These assaults have thrown open the university to society at large and demanded it become representative of that society, *conform* to that society. And conform it has. In terms of numbers nearly 50 per cent of British young people now attend university. In the 1970s and 1980s, just 30 to 40 years ago, fewer than 15 per cent read for undergraduate degrees. Such a quantitative change – out of all recognition – in such a short period of time has had qualitative impacts on the very nature of the university as it is now constituted. One is the further erosion of the authority of the liberal humanities as no longer being thought *suitable* for the majority of the new students, drawn from different cultural backgrounds and not always interested in the views of dead white men. Nor are these great numbers of students imagined to have the time or the *luxury* for such self-indulgent pursuits as the humanities. According to Stefan Collini, in 2009 just 60,000 students in the UK read English Literature, 293,000 were studying medicine (the majority nurses now that nursing care requires a degree), and 330,000 taking business studies and accountancy. The university in this sense is no more than a training ground for a life of working for the state in the form of the N.H.S., Britain's largest employer, or the corporate sector. In the 1930s, 80–90 per cent of undergraduates read humanities at just 21 universities. Today it is only 11 per cent in some 130 higher education institutions (Collini 2012: 32). In between, society has largely abandoned its support for the ideals of a liberal education.

An extensive body of literature – including this volume and its predecessor – covers the ways in which the contemporary university fails to live up to its foundational ideals. Book after book has lamented the death, demise, or decline of the university and the closing of the Western life of the mind. The problems are well-known, deep-set, and need little rehearsal: the deconstruction of the authority of the canon, of Western civilisation, of the professor; the explosion of the curriculum into specialisms and studies of every kind; the erosion of academic freedom through the loss of tenure, in politically-correct speech codes, in self-censorship for fear of giving offense, or 'triggering' coddled students; the relentless pressure to meet objectives and bureaucratic targets that are in no way academic, such as reviving the economy, levelling out social inequality and making students happy citizens. The university – having deconstructed what it was once and now no longer able to answer the existential question of what it *is* – expends its energies in trying to find a role for itself. The arguments are familiar: the academy is *for* increasing social mobility; it is *for* training citizens; it is preparing students with critical thinking skills *for* a future that we cannot predict; it is preparing young people *for* a global economy; it is *for* eliminating racism, sexism, homophobia, Islamophobia, transphobia, phobiaphobia, and prejudice in whatever form today's fevered imaginariums of offence can conjure. The university, so adrift from its foundations, spends its time in a continual and endless process of re*form*ation.

The university has turned itself into a place where fear of any kind simply will not be allowed and, therefore, has zero tolerance for any opinion that might give offence. The university has turned from being a space of freedom, a little *edgy*, to being a provider of safe spaces for students, a place that ensures young minds are never challenged, provoked, or offended. Instead of access to freedom and truth, it offers beanbags, puppies, and whale song: a comforting relativized echo chamber of untutored ignorance and narcissistic, self-regarding prejudice. *The university is dead. Long live the diversity*.

The prohibition of offence on campus is a straightforward repudiation of academic freedom. The banning of views deemed offensive by student political committees is now routine in America and Britain. It can extend to the destruction of academic careers in punishment for thought-crime, as in the case of Larry Summers at Harvard or Tim Hunt at University College London (Bilefsky 2015). University lecturers now routinely self-censor to avoid the ever-vigilant, politically correct campus zealots who are allowed, indeed often encouraged, to operate as a form of religious thought-police, apparently a welcome corrective to hundreds of years of unexamined, unearned, and *unchecked* elitist privilege. Universities, so-called, have become homes to bad faith, continuing to carry on as if nothing fundamental has changed despite their own self-denial, self-repudiation, and self-hatred. Academics rarely believe in what they are doing anymore. They have lost faith, and where they have avoided coming clean with themselves about that it is only by dint of throwing themselves into the 'sciences' in the most general sense, both the hard and the social sciences, subjects in which their apparent objectivity, their apparent relevance to the real, can serve as a cloak for a betrayal of the ideals of academic humanism.

Of course, universities have failed to live up to their ideals before. They have been socially elitist as well as just academically elitist. They have often been sleepy, complacent backwaters, every bit as much maybe as they have been bastions of brave challenges to social conformity, prejudice, and error. Western society too, of course, has failed to live up to its ideals. Instead of Kant's perpetual peace we have had revolutions, world wars, and the Holocaust. Instead of Enlightenment universalism we have had empire, totalitarianism, and racial thinking. In response, we have rejected the ideals themselves rather than tried ever harder to realise them. In disgust at what we can do, in fear of what we can be, we are in danger of settling for what we are, in demanding respect and recognition for the brute fact of being here.

The death of idealism has meant the destruction of the real university. There continue of course to be universities – in name – all across the world, more and more of them, temporary homes to ever-increasing numbers of students drawn from ever-widening and ever-more-diverse walks of life. These universities may look much like they did before. Some of the students may even read whole books. But these universities lack reality. They lack substance. They are universities in appearance only. They are post-universities, universities that no longer have a point.

Few accounts of the end of the university have compelling suggestions for how to move forward nor any inspiring vision of what the future might hold beyond McUniversity. When suggestions are made, they are often just technical in nature (internet and social media to the rescue) or further undermine the already shattered authority of the professor in favour of learner-centric models of education (the flipped classroom). Two fundamental problems need tackled head on if there is to be any future for the university. The first is the access agenda. The second is relativist epistemology. To put it less politely, the two problems we face are anarchy and nihilism.

Anarchy in the sense that the university has become a free-for-all with the only freedom on offer being a freedom from ever being told what you think is wrong, a freedom from ever being challenged, a freedom from education. The relentless and politicised drive to give access to all regardless of academic ability results in years of boredom for students who are sold a pup: sitting through vocational training courses masquerading as higher learning. The only sure outcome of this is a deep cynicism on the part of students as to the value of education, if not complete indifference to knowledge, beauty, and truth. The university will not be resurrected through initiatives to make it ever more accessible to society as a whole or more relevant. These are the measures that have killed it; applying more of the same will not bring it back to life nor recreate that ideal model of society.

Nihilism in the sense that relativism of knowledge means that, in the end, nothing really matters. The university ends up lacking any point, deprived of its objective of explaining the truths that underlie the way things appear to us. If the way things appear to me is as valid as the way they appear to you, then there is no direction of travel we can share. In the face of nihilism, it is not possible to turn back the clock and simply reassert the superiority of Enlightenment universalism, of the Western tradition, blithely ignoring the reality of the dissipation of the authority of that tradition. To pretend otherwise, however valiantly, is to overlook the extent to which the university today has become reactive and, increasingly, reactionary. Reactive in the sense that, having lost its connection with the past, it has no choice but to react to a present it is powerless to influence. Whatever the needs of the moment, the university rushes to supply them with new curricula, more vocational courses in the latest thing. Reactionary in the sense that, having discarded universalism and individualism alike, no longer believing that my reason and your reason can come to a shared truth, the university has become antisocial if not opposed to the possibility of civilisation as such. Believing in the radical incommensurability of my culture and your culture, the nihilistic university can no longer recognise my freedom and your freedom because to do so would be to allow conflict. As a result it cannot allow us to socialise freely. Hence the safe spaces of the inconsequential soft play university. Hence, intolerance of anything except nonjudgementalism. Hence, if I take offence to *The Merchant of Venice*, then you don't get to read it either. Hence, signed consent forms and the legalisation of everyday life. Hence, the therapeutic culture which sees students as objects, with behaviours to be controlled, problems to be managed.

Against all this the university needs to be rethought from first principles and refounded. We need to establish new institutions based on a root and branch rethinking of the mission and purpose of a university. We can and should of course argue for treating students as students rather than lifelong learners, we should bring back reading lists of great books, and we should argue for subjects rather than the pick-and-mix of interdisciplinary modularity. But the fundamental principle at stake is academic freedom, and so any experiments – and experimentation and risk-taking of all kinds is precisely what we should be encouraging – in education can make no compromise when it comes to institutional autonomy and the freedom of the members of these institutions. In any educational establishment worthy of the name *liberal*, the freedom to criticise should be, irony to one side, compulsory. No progress towards truth can possibly be made without the freedom to disagree and to judge for oneself. We must demand that students make value judgements and give their reasons and be prepared to defend them. And that they be prepared to listen to the judgements of others – even to those of their elders and betters – and respond to them with reason rather than emotion. To do otherwise is to keep the young in a fantasy world, cuddled away from any inconvenient truth. It is to never allow their lives to start.

In addition to academic freedom, a resolute commitment to quality, even at the expense of equality, is desperately needed. Not all students are created equal, not all of us have what it takes to be academics. It is even possible that not everyone wants to be a college don. Nor are all things equally true, nor all civilisations equally valid, nor indeed of equal historical importance. New universities must be unashamedly elitist in their commitment to academic excellence. More broadly, the best thing we could do for many students in the contemporary university is stop pretending that three years there is going to do them any good whatsoever. They would be better served by staying at home and reading the Western canon, for free, on their Kindles.

Above all, in the end we need a fresh beginning. We need to find a way to create a sacred oasis in the middle of the desert of the real. And that means re-establishing the university on its original footing: as a model of how society should be and as a vehicle for moving us closer to that ideal. New universities must task themselves with coming up with new models of society, finding new answers to the question of how to live together. They must engage in a relentless critique of what society actually is, must rip away the appearances of things and lay bare how they really are. Yes, culture and the liberal arts must once more be at the heart of the university. Yes, we must mine the thinkers and the great books of the past for clues and guides how to advance. Yes, we must find ways to reject instrumentalism in all its forms and argue why education is an end in itself, a divine activity. But none of this will be enough without the courage of those coming together in a community dedicated to the pursuit of truth so as to afford us a mirror of the process whereby society creates itself and to act as a reminder of how the university is – at its best – an ideal real.

References

Bilefsky, D. (2015) Women Respond to Nobel Laureate's 'Trouble with Girls', *The New York Times*, 11 June: http://www.nytimes.com/2015/06/12/world/europe/tim-hunt-nobel-laureate-resigns-sexist-women-female-scientists.html?_r=0 (Accessed 18 August 2016).

Collini, S. (2012) *What Are Universities For?* London: Penguin.

Newman, J.H. (1907) *The Idea of a University*, London: Longmans, Green and Company.

Watson, P. (2010) *The German Genius*, New York, NY: Simon and Schuster.

5

BEYOND THE SECULAR UNIVERSITY

Clare Hornsby and Sebastian Morello

The crisis

It has been noted for some time by those concerned with the direction and purpose of present-day education that the academy is in crisis. This is illustrated by the fact that the notion of a 'core curriculum' is now centred on the STEM disciplines almost exclusively (science, technology, engineering and mathematics). These receive the most external funding and government support, both for departments and for the students. These subjects, for all their nobility, are ordered toward utility. Even those more speculative disciplines, science and mathematics for example, for which a case can be made that they are foundational for the attainment of wisdom, are now imparted within a pedagogy which emphasises an instrumental finality, as opposed to knowledge for the sake of human cultivation and civilisation.

Secondary schools and colleges, even the UK's best elite schools, now tend to educate pupils not with a view to forming the person, and the minds of such persons, but to produce those who will succeed when it comes to employability and ultimately achieve financial goals. Indeed, when secondary schools open their doors to university promotional teams at sixth form level, the word on everyone's lips at these careers fairs is, perhaps understandably, employability. Students are not so much seen as persons but rather functionaries being prepared to fit into a future slot in a global, money-making corporation. Universities in turn promote themselves as institutions which can prepare a young person to fill such a slot.

Martin Stephen, the former headmaster of one such elite school – St Paul's in London – describes the problem in the following way:

> There is a basic problem with the concept of liberal education, which is that for any state or parent-funded school pragmatism will be a bigger driver than liberalism. One definition of a liberal education is that it is an education that

allows pupils to be exposed to the widest possible range of influences and opinions, seeking to develop the pupil's own judgement on those issues rather than impose or preach an Establishment view ... a liberal education is a game with no boundaries, but the urge of all but the most enlightened governments to slap border controls on at every opportunity condemns the two to a longstanding war.

(Stephen 2009: 2)

The issue of utility-based education has even made its mark on some liberal arts colleges and universities. Founded in reaction to that current, they have nevertheless failed to resist the discourse of utility wholeheartedly, proposing to prepare students to 'tackle the challenges of employability today'. This hardly suggests that the pursuit of wisdom is at the heart of the curriculum; it appears that wisdom is a luxury rather than a necessity. Nevertheless it should be recalled that liberal arts education has always been a rigorous training of the mind and therefore produced great leaders, teachers and public servants. The current crisis is due to the abandonment of wisdom as the aim of education, and the shunning of the transcendental attributes that give human life meaning: Truth, Goodness and Beauty.

There is at present no tertiary institution offering a fully integrated course in the traditional liberal arts in the UK. The syllabuses of most humanities programmes remain markedly deficient, addressing neither fundamental questions of the nature and purpose of the human person nor his dignity and worth from a theological perspective. Such programmes do not attempt to integrate the teaching of arts and sciences in a cultural context but rather prefer to create artificial divisions in learning, replacing real intellectual challenges with 'teaching to the exam'. Consequently, at undergraduate level, in the race for professionalism, students specialise early, following a now-established convention which states that education is successful in direct proportion to its compliance with the interests of the student, often assumed to be fully formed before the course even begins. There is a need to return to true education, one which requires the acceptance of certain fundamental distinctions and a recognition of the order among the objects of thought.

Our civilisation is not one primarily of utility; indeed, there cannot be such a thing as a civilisation of utility even if practical disciplines hold an indispensable place in its establishment (see Pieper 1963: 53). Our civilisation is one of revealed religion, wisdom and law; in other words, we are heirs to the legacies of Jerusalem, Athens and Rome. The liberal arts are the way in which we have always formed ourselves in this great heritage, and these arts are, as O'Hear and Sidwell point out, always a 'tradition more than a pedagogical theory' (O'Hear and Sidwell 2009: 6). We must, if we are to recover our civilisation, rediscover the liberal arts, and remain faithful to them.

The meaning of the liberal arts

The liberal arts form the central educational tradition of Western civilisation. Born among the philosophers of fifth-century Athens, carried forward by statesmen and public figures of the Roman republic and empire, it was ultimately through the Catholic Church that the tradition flourished across Europe and survived into the modern era. Sometimes its survival was precarious; Alcuin of York was a rare champion of the liberal arts in the eighth century, called by the Holy Roman Emperor Charlemagne to educate his court and, as a result, spread culture across Western Europe. Over the centuries, scholars patronised by popes and secular courts, those active in the monastic tradition of Benedict of Nursia and later in the universities, helped to preserve and gradually re-establish this system of education at the heart of Christendom. The Christian belief in a God of reason, and in man made in the image of God, was a natural complement to the rational inquiry of the Greeks; in the words of Pope Benedict XVI, 'The encounter between the Biblical message and Greek thought did not happen by chance' (Pope Benedict XVI 2006: 6). Together, they provided the foundation for the cultural achievements of Europe through the Middle Ages, the Renaissance, and into the modern age.

Liberal arts education does not focus on one subject in isolation but rather emphasises breadth. Also, it sees all knowledge as connected, each aspect informing the whole. The core of this education has traditionally been the seven liberal arts: the disciplines of language – grammar, logic and rhetoric – as well as the arts of number, including geometry and arithmetic. Philosophy and then theology came to be the crowning disciplines of liberal arts education, the subjects which enable students to understand the relationship that all studies have to what we can know about ourselves, the world and ultimately about God. It is this point that holds the key to a renewal of education in its true sense. As Rowan Williams said in his Oxford sermon of June 2004:[1]

> The university was, as I put it earlier, a cell of the Body of Christ. The Christian revelation was not thought to be a series of truths only; it was an action that created a form of human life together reflecting God's purpose for humanity: the propositions of revelation were not given so as to be digested by individual minds with no further end in view; they were the instructions for shaping and ordering holy lives, lives in which the rational divine image was becoming more visible.

Recognising the gulf which separates contemporary society from that of medieval and early modern Europe when belief in God was the cornerstone assumption on which it was based, one way in which we can access that world and recalibrate education to its ultimate purpose of wisdom is through the study of history, itself not a traditional liberal art nor even traditional discipline of study. It was not until the twentieth century that history as a discipline was taught in universities. It was thought that the study of history belonged to recreation and leisure and should be that with which all cultured people are familiar, a shared background. Familiarity with history was seen then to be an essential part of being cultured. So, in promoting true culture today, the teaching of history, especially the history of Christian culture and ideas, should be central to liberal arts education: 'It is therefore of vital importance to maintain the key position of the liberal arts college in the university and to save the liberal arts course from further disintegration. And it is with these ends in view that I have made my suggestions for the study of Christian culture as a means of integration and unity' (Dawson 1963: 103). This culture is integrated by examination of its effects through the ages, the historical perspective. History – cultural, artistic, political – forms a web that binds us and our activities across the centuries. It also provides students with the training ground through which the analytical approach can be developed and refined.

A contemporary liberal arts education should embody a unique coherence and integration; such a way of learning introduces students to the joy of seeking knowledge for its own sake, equipping them to participate in the intellectual current running through Western civilisation. This amounts to an education which enriches the whole of a student's future life. John Henry Newman wrote in *The Idea of a University* that by participating in a liberal arts education, 'a habit of mind is formed which lasts through life, of which the attributes are freedom, equitableness, calmness, moderation, and wisdom' (Newman [1907] 2001 Discourse 6: 101). In a true liberal arts education all studies must be in harmony; the lesser sciences preparing the student for the greater and more challenging work of philosophy and theology, acting as means of illumination and clarification of their complexities. In such learning the greatest minds in Western civilisation are to be read, analysed and discussed not only for historical and cultural reasons but because they represent the best attempts to understand things in themselves (based on our shared experience) as well as the most direct path toward attainment of the intellectual virtues. The finest works of human genius should be held to be of the highest value because they touch the truth. Education is in itself a hollow concept unless this basic orientation to truth is recognised and retained; the teacher must lead the student, to use Newman's phrase, *ex umbris et imaginibus in veritatem* – out of shadows and images into truth.

Christian wisdom and cultural renewal

Roger Scruton, in his essay on T. S. Eliot as conservative mentor, comments on the personal impact of culture and how the loss of it leads to barbarism, which 'ensues, not because people have lost their skills and scientific knowledge, nor is it averted by retaining those things' (Scruton 2004). Scruton's phrase points toward the jargon terminology used to define what our pupils and students have to be taught, defined as 'transferable skills'. In truth, it cannot be about transferable skills; rather, what we are concerned with is the enrichment of the whole person.

The liberal arts ground people in true culture by bringing together reflections on the past and the present from historians of art and literature, theologians, philosophers and scientists, which can throw light on our humanity and our society. In short, such an education is ordered toward the preservation and regeneration of European culture. Even presupposing no personal or institutional commitment to Christian faith, such an enterprise is impossible independent of an embracing of the Christian intellectual heritage. Concerned with this very issue, Eliot stated the following:

An individual European may not believe that the Christian faith is true and yet what he says and makes and does will all spring out of his heritage of Christian culture and depend on that culture for its meaning. Only Christian culture could have produced a Voltaire or a Nietzsche. I do not believe that the culture of Europe could survive the complete disappearance of the Christian faith. And I am convinced of that, not merely because I am a Christian myself, but as a student of social biology. If Christianity goes, the whole of our culture goes. Then you must start painfully again, and you cannot put on a new culture ready-made. You must wait for the grass to grow to feed the sheep to give the wool out of which your new coat will be made. You must pass through many centuries of barbarism. We should not live to see the new culture, nor would our great-great-great grandchildren, and if we did, not one of us would be happy in it.

(Eliot 1948: 120)

Eliot's words suggest that what is required is more than some benevolent respect for the Christian heritage as one among many; rather, we must conserve it but with the conviction that this is essential for the future of our civilisation, and be convinced of this because we believe that its content is true. The true liberal arts education, by definition, must be Christian: it grew from the incorporation of the truths of ancient philosophy within the context of Christian Europe. It was protected by the saints, fostered in the cathedral schools, disseminated by monastic scribes, and applied in noble and royal courts throughout Christendom. There are several reasons why we assert that a true liberal arts education needs to have this dimension. As liberal arts education is to form the whole person, it must form the virtues, and that necessarily includes those known as the theological virtues of faith, hope and charity; secondly, Christian revelation is the proper object of theology, and its incorporation into the liberal arts curriculum provides the certainty necessary to the study of the other disciplines; and finally, as liberal arts education aims at cultural renewal, one must know intimately the *cultus* at the heart of culture. Let us examine these three points.

This form of education implies the formation of the virtues, primarily the intellectual virtues, but also all those habits which order man toward his proper finality. In Catholic anthropology, man is understood to be born wounded and incomplete due to original sin; indeed, this is why in Catholic theology (unlike in Protestant theology) grace is believed to build upon human nature and bring it to perfection, not merely 'hide' human brokenness. This freely given gift of grace enters into the life of the Christian and enables him to partake of the Divine Nature, and such a life implies the cultivation of the theological virtues. These virtues also presuppose man's capacity for the virtue of religion, i.e., that natural virtue which inclines man to give to God the worship He is due as the first principle of all that is. The point here is a simple one: the liberal arts are ordered toward the education of the whole person, but due to original sin there is no 'whole person' independent of the Christian mysteries. In turn, if the liberal arts are truly to fulfil their purpose, they must belong to a Christian education.

Regarding the second point, as stated above, along with philosophy, theology is the crowning discipline in the liberal arts curriculum. Theology is not the same as 'religious studies', for theology is strictly speaking the 'science of God', i.e. applying reason to grasp the intelligibility of God's own revelation of Himself. One could argue that theology taught only as a *historical* discipline has a key role in a liberal education, as it gives the students the conceptual tools to understand Western civilisation. A basic knowledge of Christianity is indispensable for reading the monuments – literary and artistic – which this civilisation has given us. However, this would not suffice for an adequate understanding; rather, it is necessary to be engaged in theological enquiry from within the Christian and, ideally, Catholic tradition. No doubt, historical theology or religious studies should have a place in the liberal arts curriculum, but the Christian intelligence needs – for its own formation – theology as a *rational reflection on God's revelation, as faith seeking understanding.*

Oxford University recently revised its curriculum for the BA degree in theology – now called theology and religion – dispensing with any obligatory courses in the second and third year. Only a thin veneer of Christianity will be studied, then the student can continue in any direction. This is of course in keeping with the general trend of the humanities in the UK, moving away from a fixed curriculum to an individual combination of optional modules. In the case of theology, the consequences are dramatic. You can now obtain a BA degree in theology without having studied at any depth the formative first centuries of Christian history, or indeed the pivotal sixteenth century. The changes are justified with reference to 'religious and cultural diversification in the UK', but as a recent article in *The Times Higher Education* suggests, 'scholarly approaches to research could be at the root of changes to undergraduate teaching more widely in the humanities' (Staufenberg 2016). That is to say, approaches to research are reflecting the narrow interests of new generations of lecturers and the obligation of these to assist their institutions in gaining more funding – via a high score on the Research Excellence Framework – rather than fulfilling the needs or even the expectations of students.

Christian – most specifically Catholic – theology has much to offer in this situation. In his Regensburg address, Pope Benedict was keen to point toward the concept of *logos* at the centre of Christian faith in God. *Logos* can be translated as 'word', but also as 'reason', meaning, 'order'. The God who is *logos* guarantees the intelligibility of the world, the intelligibility of our existence. The recognition of the God who is *logos* demands that the object remain primary and one's subjectivity remain secondary. Whereas modernity is characterised by a narrowing of reason (limiting it to empirical and scientific inquiry), the Christian proclamation keeps the breadth of reason alive, allowing for speculation arising from abstract questions and enabling proper perennial metaphysical and ethical issues to be engaged with, in depth. Such emphasis on the primacy of the object also marks an antidote to the culture of feeling, which wants to make universities 'safe spaces' in which certain topics can no longer be freely discussed. Without the approach of faith, theology quickly degenerates into comparative studies in religion. As Newman noted, 'religious truth is not only a portion, but a condition of general knowledge. To blot it out is nothing short ... of unravelling the web of university teaching' (Newman [1907] 2001 Discourse 3: 70).

On the third point, it is notable that the words *culture* and *cult* have the same etymological root: *cultus*. We can say that true culture is the expression of the sanctified human community. When we look at the various forms of high culture – among them art, dance, music, theatre, literature – we find that what characterises all these natural human achievements is that they reach their summit in their assumption into Christian culture. Christianity safeguards culture and prevents it from descending into barbarism.

As Josef Pieper in *Leisure: The Basis of Culture* noted, religion – cult – is that which man pursues for no other reason than to possess that toward which it is ordered, God Himself (see Pieper 1963: 65–74). Culture has its foundation in leisure; that is to say, in the sphere of human activity, culture is as far from utility as one can get. In everyday life, culture is sanctified by religion, and work transcends any instrumentalist aim that it might have. It is for this reason that the liberal arts, in their aim to introduce students to philosophy and theology, must be completely committed to a rigorous study of the arts and culture, specifically Christian culture. Any liberal arts enterprise which does not focus intensely on music, art, literature and the general cultivation of the virtue of *eutrapelia* – the discovery of that which pertains to leisure – is missing something essential to the educational formation. And any attempt to explain Western culture and civilisation without reference to Christianity is an impossible task.

Benedictus liberal arts in London

At the beginning of 2011 the decision was taken to form a charitable trust that would be the starting point for the foundation of a new initiative in tertiary education for the UK. The aim was to found an independent college offering a single programme of studies in the traditional liberal arts, including history, languages and the art of Western civilisation; the whole course embracing the Catholic intellectual and cultural tradition. Phase One of the vision is to offer a certificate in the liberal arts, a one-year introductory course made up of three terms that can be studied as a whole or individually by international students. Phase Two is to develop, resource and gain accreditation for a three-year BA course and offer students the chance to take a liberal arts degree at a dedicated institution, something that is almost unknown in the UK higher education market. Benedictus is both a new beginning and a return to tradition, the first institution of its kind in the UK. It is a new concept and marks the revival of a way of studying that dates back many centuries; one that has not lost its original power to open minds and sharpen the intellect. The proof of the viability of this concept has been given by the success of summer schools offering a taste of this specially created curriculum to students from other institutions, held in London over the last two years.

The return to the structure and richness of a liberal arts curriculum envisages a single, dedicated course that serves as an initiation into the great conversation of Western civilisation. Whilst faithful to the Catholic intellectual tradition, students of

any culture or religious background would be welcomed. Centred on the development of the whole person and affirming the principle that education is the joyful
pursuit of wisdom, it is essential to offer the sort of tutorial experience normally
reserved for Oxford and Cambridge combined with a programme of lectures and in-
depth seminars. Wherever possible the course books should be original texts so that
students will learn directly from the greatest minds in history and discuss the same
important questions as they did. Based in London, students will be able to take full
advantage of the cultural riches of the capital, including frequent visits to art galleries,
museums and concerts as part of their learning experience. Above all, Benedictus will
offer membership in a community of scholarship, a place where students can develop
critical thinking and intellectual versatility in dialogue with a highly qualified faculty.

St. Benedict and Blessed John Henry Newman

The inspiration for this educational initiative comes from two great figures in particular.
First is Benedict of Nursia, the founder of Western monasticism. The son of a Roman
nobleman, he was born amid the chaos of the end of the Western Roman Empire. He
was eager to foster a new era of Christian faith, culture and scholarship, bringing the
gifts of the Church to wider society. Benedict wrote a rule for his monastic order and in
it he insisted on the importance of learning. The Benedictine monasteries and convents
both preserved and enlarged Europe's cultural inheritance. We owe much to the
libraries of the Benedictine abbeys, with their dedicated scribes, for conserving the great
works of the West; without this heritage, modern scholars would not know many of
the great books of the ancient world. The monasteries supported the education of both
men and women, reaching out from the abbey walls to teach children of the nearby
regions. Thomas Aquinas began his education at the Benedictine abbey of Monte
Cassino (where Benedict had been abbot many centuries before), south of Rome.
Aquinas went on to do more than anyone else to unite Christian doctrine with the
Greek tradition of inquiry exemplified by Aristotle.

Second is John Henry Newman. In *The Idea of a University* Newman continues
to inspire debate amongst educators, both Christian and agnostic (see Kennedy,
Chapter 4 in this volume). He held that the university must be, before anything
else, a community of seekers, engaging in the intellectual pursuit for no other
reason than out of love for the truth. As a great promoter of the liberal arts, he
believed that the university must teach students 'to think and to reason and to
compare and to discriminate and to analyse' (Newman [1907] 2001 Discourse 7:
166). Today the academy is dominated by pressure to specialise. Newman, however, held that narrow specialisation gave rise to narrow minds and postulated that
students should have a solid foundation in all areas of inquiry.

The Benedictus pedagogy

Amongst the features of the Benedictus approach to the liberal arts is a commitment to maintaining small classes, focussing on primary sources, and facilitating

learning and insight through discussion and dialectic. From the time of Socrates, education has been based on dialogue guided by a teacher. While lectures, seminars and essay writing all play a part, liberal arts education must always be centred on the discussion of primary texts so that students become familiar with what the masters taught, not merely with what others have said about what the masters taught. As Aquinas wrote, 'non respicias a quo audias, sed quidquid boni dicatur'.[2] Active discussion remains the best way to draw students in to participate. Such engagement enhances the powers of reason, analysis and articulation. In this course, the tutors will highlight the connections that exist between the philosophy, literature and arts of each specific historical period and encourage the students to make cross-references between areas of study, enriching their cultural hinterland.

However, what really distinguishes Benedictus from other liberal arts colleges in the US or on the European continent is its engagement with the serious study of art. To fully grasp the great Western intellectual tradition, it is not enough to rely on written texts alone; material culture should be embraced on an equal level with the intellectual since it is an integral part of the context in which key philosophical and theological texts were created. It is a principle of liberal arts education that knowledge is one. This unity of knowledge demands that all the disciplines answer one to the other, and an intelligent curriculum responds to this principle, which also in turn responds to the differing strengths of the members of the student body. Thus, evidencing the links between, for example, biology and printing, between painting and philosophy, between architecture and music theory, is fruitful not only in itself, but the results of any such integrated inquiry have a greater impact than the constituent disciplines studied separately.

It is obvious that if a particular historical period is taken – for example, the mid- to late-fifteenth century in Florence – the evidence we have of the cultural and intellectual life of the period will be diverse. Without fully rejecting the purist approach of reading texts for themselves in an intellectual isolation which concentrates the mind on the 'big questions' free from distractions, students who look at the breadth of both material and intellectual production of a period are enlightened by the examination of its life as a whole, not fragmenting the past by imposing on it an anachronistic division into 'subjects'. These varied cultural productions give not only a glimpse of the incredible richness and rewards of studying that period *qua* history but enable the student to experience for themselves the unity of knowledge. Art – studied in small groups in galleries, museums and on site – will no longer remain on the sidelines, considered only as an entertaining diversion from the work of reading; perceived as more demanding, it will take its rightful place at the centre of scholarly inquiry. By examining the great works of art, architecture, music and literature, and by researching the role of art in society, we enrich our world and enhance our sense of beauty. Many works were created as part of the artist's search for truth, and specifically in the Christian context, art was made in the service of God: *ad majorem Dei gloriam*. The serious study of art, therefore, is central to any fully comprehensive programme of study: 'Truth has two attributes – beauty and power; and while Useful Knowledge is the possession of truth as powerful, Liberal Knowledge is the apprehension of it as beautiful' (Newman [1907] 2001 Discourse 9: 2).

Conclusion

The intellectual tradition of the liberal arts proposed here aims to preserve the same tradition which gave us great scholars like Augustine, Boethius, Aquinas, More and Erasmus. The inspiration behind Benedictus is that which brought forth an unrivalled richness in culture across all disciplines. Liberal arts education should not neglect the Christian and classical tradition, which is still very much present throughout the fabric of the West. Our contemporary culture seems to reject, with an ever more fervently nihilistic vigour, not only its incontestably Christian roots but also anything associated with the good, the true, the noble and the beautiful (Casey 2015). If a society is judged by its cultural outputs, the excitement generated by artists whose glaring lack of talent is compensated for by crudity, pyrotechnics, obscenity or kitsch is the firmest condemnation of our society. Education is often lacking in quality, and universities today increasingly seem to see their sole mission as the production of small cogs in the gears of global capitalism and consumerism. Learning for the sheer love of truth, which is the central pillar of classical education, is a concept largely reminiscent of a bygone era – yet this is precisely one of the core tenets of Benedictus.

We live in a deeply wounded culture that has lost direction and any sense of purpose outside itself. Values – ill-defined and perhaps undefinable – have replaced the virtues in public life. The mission of the Benedictus liberal arts curriculum is to awaken in its students an awareness of beauty, a desire to seek the good and the true through an experience of the beautiful. This should naturally lead to a recognition of that which is transcendent and perennial. It is imperative to develop and nurture aspirations and ideals that truly reflect the high calling, the vocation of man, that orient culture to its true purpose. Benedictus is a conduit through which a real recovery of our heritage can be made possible; it is clear that there is a need for a reconnection with that heritage in order to make it part of the contemporary educational experience. An education that offers to embrace fully the challenge of the pursuit of wisdom, not shying away from truth as an aim, is clearly counter-cultural; we believe that the clarity of the message will nevertheless strengthen its appeal.

Notes

1 Oxford University Commemoration Day Sermon, Sunday, 20 June 2004, given at the University Church of St Mary the Virgin, Oxford: http://www.benedictus.org.uk/Resources/RowanWilliamsTalk.pdf.
2 *Epistle to Brother John*, 'listen not to who is speaking but what good they speak'.

References

Casey, J. P. (2015) Closing Remarks, Benedictus Forum, London 2015: http://www.benedictus.org.uk/Resources/JeanPierreCasey.pdf (accessed 19 August 2016).

Dawson, C. (1963) *The Crisis of Western Education*, Washington, DC: The Catholic University of America Press.

Eliot, T. S. (1948) *Notes Towards the Definition of Culture*, London: Faber and Faber.

O'Hear, A. and Sidwell, M. (eds.) (2009) *The School of Freedom*, Exeter and Charlottesville, VA: Imprint Academic.

Newman, J. H. ([1907] 2001) *The Idea of a University*, London: Longmans, Green and Company: http://www.newmanreader.org/works/idea/ (accessed 19 August 2016).

Pieper, J. (1963) *Leisure: The Basis of Culture*, London: Random House.

Pope Benedict XVI (2006) Faith, reason and the university: memories and reflections, University of Regensburg Lecture, 15 September: http://w2.vatican.va/content/benedict-xvi/en/speeches/2006/september/documents/hf_ben-xvi_spe_20060912_university-regensburg.html (accessed 19 August 2016).

Scruton, R. (2004) T. S. Eliot as conservative mentor, *Intercollegiate Review* (Orientation Issue) Fall 2003/Spring 2004: https://home.isi.org/t-s-eliot-conservative-mentor (accessed 19 August 2016).

Sidwell, M. (2009) The strange death of liberal education, in O'Hear, A. and Sidwell, M. (eds.) *The School of Freedom*, Exeter and Charlottesville, VA: Imprint Academic: 1–3.

Staufenberg, J. (2016) Modern humanities teaching: brought on by the chicken or the egg? *Times Higher Education*, 21 March: https://www.timeshighereducation.com/news/modern-humanities-teaching-brought-on-by-the-chicken-or-the-egg (accessed 19 August 2016).

Stephen, M. (2009) Foreword, in O'Hear, A. and Sidwell, M. (eds.) *The School of Freedom*, Exeter and Charlottesville, VA: Imprint Academic.

Williams, R. (2004) Oxford University Commemoration Day sermon, Oxford, 20 June: http://www.benedictus.org.uk/Resources/RowanWilliamsTalk.pdf (accessed 16 August 2016).

6

BEYOND CENSORSHIP

Toward a Republic of Science

Adam Kissel

No one is King of the Republic of Science. And even if theology were Queen of the Sciences, as tradition holds, she has almost entirely abdicated her role in U.S. higher education. No one is in charge, and we like it that way. While professors around the world risk their lives promoting knowledge – the internationally renowned organization Scholars at Risk has hundreds of examples – scholars in America have it pretty easy.

Threats to free and open inquiry in the United States, however, do exist – plenty of them. Yet, these threats are not well understood, with the result that those who advocate greater freedom in higher education are often fighting the wrong battles. Speech codes, censorship zones, and disinvitations of campus speakers are pervasive in U.S. higher education and are commonly decried in U.S. media (see Lukianoff 2014 and Lukianoff and Haidt 2015). To be sure, such individual outrages must be challenged. But attention to the structural forces against free and open inquiry is almost entirely missing from public discourse.

Missing in particular is the observation that the public funding and administration of higher education is not neutral. Government schools and government funds come with government administrators and government agendas and ideologies. The state's billions of dollars often come not with strings attached but with iron bars.

And the structural threats come not merely from government. The philosopher Immanuel Kant recognized an enduring conflict between those who search for truth and authorities of all kinds who claim to know the truth already. In *The Conflict of the Faculties* ([1798] 1992), Kant sees that the fundamental problem for freedom of thought is not church vs. state. Both church and state, ideological powers and government actors alike, interfere with free inquiry. What is more, Kant sees, professional associations claim disciplinary authority over members whose ideas get out of line.

After a brief elaboration of the value of free inquiry, this chapter provides examples of these oppressive powers in the United States: ideology, state, and professional associations. The chapter concludes with recommendations for proactive reform.

Defenses of free speech and open inquiry

Free thought and free inquiry need defense because, by nature, they threaten to uncover something that differs from the status quo, and the status quo has stakeholders. Open inquiry and free speech need defense because, by nature, they threaten to expose observers to ideas that might challenge the status quo.

Defending free and open inquiry against the stakeholders of the status quo is not easy because so much might be at stake. As a result of free thought and free speech, an entire religion might fall. The foundations of the state might crumble. The fundamentals of a profession might prove false. In innumerable ways, the status quo might prove to be a false stasis.

The job of defending free inquiry is easier where respect for challenges to the status quo is baked into the values of the stakeholders. For philosopher Michael Polanyi, the Republic of Science is one such place (1962). While maintaining scientific discipline, the scientific enterprise in a Republic of Science depends on serious engagement with new ideas. Although well-grounded new ideas do not take hold right away, and although academic periodicals censor and curate, new and radical ideas are, in principle, tolerated. Cranks are not prevented from exploring their ideas, even though these people and their ideas rarely get much attention. Science advances while each person learns from what others are doing nearby and across academia, adjusting accordingly.

For author Jonathan Rauch, liberal society is another such place ([1995] 2013). Not only in academia's practice of "liberal science" but also in a free society, new ideas are tolerated because no authority is supposed to have the final word on the truth, and anyone's idea might be incorporated into the culture's common stock. As in the Republic of Science, the liberal society does not require relativism. In the mix of traditions that comprise the modern American Republic, everyone is, in principle, free to think and say what they want, but government representatives of the people still make binding decisions once everyone, in principle, has been heard. Society advances while each person learns from what others are doing nearby and across the nation, adjusting accordingly.

The ideas of a Republic of Science and of "liberal science" in a free society have predecessors in poet John Milton's metaphor of a broken statue we are all putting back together ([1644] 1918), philosopher David Hume's metaphor of international free trade in ideas ([1742] 1987), philosopher John Stuart Mill's metaphor of spectators overlooking a battlefield of ideas that is open to all comers ([1859] 1879), and novelist H. G. Wells' metaphor, popularized by United States Supreme Court Justice Oliver Wendell Holmes, of a free marketplace of ideas where every idea has its chance to gain market share (Wells 1918; Holmes 1919). And much earlier, theologian and rhetorical master Saint Augustine argued that just as the ancient Israelites had remade Egyptian gold for their own purposes, Christians should feel comfortable incorporating what is true from pagan learning into their own understanding ([397] 1996: Book II).

In each case, the point is that we do not have enough truth on our own to ban the utterance of any idea or to ban any person from the opportunity to contribute to our joint search for knowledge. No idea is utterly worthless since, at worst, refuting it helps reinforce our understanding of why some other idea is better.

Threats beyond McDonaldization

Not everyone sees the situation this way. The McDonaldization of the contemporary university has filled colleges with bottom-line bureaucrats who tell parents, students, and legislators that the point of postsecondary education is to prepare young adults for higher-paying jobs. Critical thinking, it seems, is for the purpose of problem-solving in diverse corporate teams. American companies, meanwhile, are forced to restrict speech by the Equal Employment Opportunity Commission, which will not let them tolerate First Amendment-level free speech in almost any workplace. Students who need to be prepared for adult life had better learn to be team players who keep their wildest ideas to themselves.

But McDonaldized bureaucracy is far from the worst influence against free expression on campus. First among these have been church and state or, in modern terms, ideology and state, because those with the privilege or opportunity for great power have had much to gain or lose from manipulating inquiry. Even today, liberal values in the academy and society at large are not enough to overcome such special interests. Furthermore, university administrators and academic authorities have their own interests at stake and they, too, have been significant censors of freedom in the U.S. academy. Each group is considered in turn below.

Ideology

One example spanning four hundred years should suffice. Harvard College has been full of Puritans since 1636, even though the original Puritans have died out. Harvard's first president, Henry Dunster, was a Puritan, but he resigned in 1654 after he was judged unfit to serve because he had stopped believing in the spiritual value of infant baptism. During the controversy, the General Court of Massachusetts advised Harvard's overseers

> not to ... suffer any such to be continued in the office or place of teaching, educating, or instructing of youth or child, in the college or schools, that have manifested themselves unsound in the faith, or scandalous in their lives, and not giving due satisfaction according to the rules of Christ.
>
> *(Williams 2014: 215)*

In this generation the intolerant moralizing is the same, but the ideology is different. When Harvard Law School adopted a speech code in 1995 to keep students from "unwanted" sex-related speech, Dean Robert Clark called it "a sign of the times." In 2005, Harvard President Lawrence H. Summers resigned after he was tarred and feathered for offering a variety of explanations of why women are found less often than men at the highest reaches of the sciences. In 2011, the Harvard faculty effectively fired one of their own, Indian politician, professor, and economist Subramanian Swamy, for having written an opinion piece in India against radical Muslims in India (Silverglate 2013).

In 2012, all Harvard freshmen were pressured to sign a "kindness pledge," which would commit them

> to upholding the values of the College and to making the [dormitory] entryway and [Harvard] Yard a place where all can thrive and where the exercise of kindness holds a place on a par with intellectual attainment.
>
> *(Silverglate 2013)*

In 2012, a Harvard Law student privately emailed friends about the subject of race and intelligence without taking a position, but when Dean Martha Minow learned about it, she wrote,

> Here at Harvard Law School, we are committed to preventing degradation of any individual or group, including race-based insensitivity or hostility. The particular comment in question unfortunately resonates with old and hurtful misconceptions. As an educational institution, we are especially dedicated to exposing to the light of inquiry false views about individuals or groups.
>
> *(Silverglate 2013)*

Finally, in 2016, Harvard announced that it will blacklist members of many same-sex, off-campus social groups, banning the students from serving in leadership roles among registered student organizations on campus and even from receiving prestigious scholarships. This is not a blanket ban, of course, because special interests enjoy exceptions (Foundation for Individual Rights in Education 2016). Harvard has insisted on enforcing its latest non-negotiable values.

In each case, from 1636 to 2016, Harvard's official values have trumped fundamental freedoms. McDonaldization is a recent factor, because the recent restrictions and controversies reflect the desire to keep tuition-paying units – customers, that is, also known as students – from becoming too disturbed on the battlefield of ideas. But the larger factor in these cases is ideology combined with power: Those with different or dissenting views threaten the hegemony of the official view and the power of the people who cultivate that view. Harvard's official ideology, though it changes over the generations, demands conformity. While Harvard is far from unique among American universities in its oppression of diverse ideas – see the extensive case files of the Foundation for Individual Rights in Education – it certainly has the longest tradition of intolerance of diversity.

State

The U.S. federal and state governments, their administrative agencies, and their funding agencies together exert enormous pressure on American colleges and universities. Some of these pressures are explicit demands to conform with official government values, complete with speech restrictions. These demands come with teeth, threatening the loss of government subsidies to the schools as well as their students. Public universities face even greater pressures since they are officially agents of the state and subject to the budgetary whims of legislatures. Still other pressures arise because the government's research agendas offer billions of dollars for the research favored by government.

Official government values

The U.S. Department of Justice and the U.S. Department of Education have interpreted federal law to require colleges to enforce speech restrictions in the name of nondiscrimination. In 2013, as a result of an investigation into the University of Montana, the agencies issued a "blueprint for colleges and universities throughout the country" threatening discipline of colleges that fail to ban "unwelcome" sex-related speech (Creeley 2014).

Professors caught up in the nondiscrimination hysteria include Northwestern University professor Laura Kipnis, who faced discriminatory harassment charges because of an essay about "sexual paranoia" she had published in *The Chronicle of Higher Education* (2015a). Kipnis observes:

> What's being lost … is the liberty to publish ideas that might go against the grain or to take on risky subjects in the first place. With students increasingly regarded as customers and consumer satisfaction paramount, it's imperative to avoid creating potential classroom friction with unpopular ideas if you're on a renewable contract and wish to stay employed. Self-censorship naturally prevails. But even those with tenure fear getting caught up in some horrendous disciplinary process with ad hoc rules and outcomes; pretty much everyone now self-censors accordingly.
>
> When it comes to campus sexual politics, however, the group most constrained from speaking – even those with tenure – is men. No male academic in his right mind would write what I did.
>
> *(Kipnis 2015b)*

To avoid federal investigation and punishment, universities err on the side of censorship rather than free speech. Federal and state governments also encroach on the academic freedom of American universities through workplace laws, not just regarding unions and health insurance mandates, but also in the mandatory use of government-sanctioned pronouns when addressing employees (Hasson 2016). To avoid university investigation and punishment under the rules demanded by the government, such rules are mandated by diversity offices, human resource offices, and university counsels. To avoid internal investigation and punishment under university rules, as Kipnis argues, professors self-censor.

Furthermore, at the state level, consider the following examples:

- South Carolina meted out budgetary punishment in 2014 to two state universities that had included gay-themed books as required readings (Cohn 2014).
- Tennessee in 2016 banned the use of state funds for the University of Tennessee "to promote the use of gender neutral pronouns, to promote or inhibit the celebration of religious holidays, or to fund or support sex week [an annual sex-oriented event]" (Cohn 2016).
- On the opposite side of such moral questions from South Carolina and Tennessee, a California bill in 2016 has threatened penalties against universities, primarily Christian ones, that do not hew to the state's official morality on sexuality. A group of college presidents and religious leaders wrote in August:

> This legislation puts into principle that majoritarian beliefs are more deserving of legal protection, and that minority viewpoints are deserving of government harassment. Legislation of this nature threatens the integrity not only of religious institutions, but of any viewpoint wishing to exercise basic American freedoms, not least of which is the freedom of conscience.
>
> *(Ethics & Religious Liberty Commission 2016)*

Official government facts

Again, one pervasive example should suffice. Reasonable scientists disagree about the variety of facts and judgments summed up in the term "global warming" or, more recently, "climate change." Which parts of the planet and its atmosphere are heating or cooling and by how much? What have the recent and long-term patterns been? What research methods and data are legitimate and reliable? How much better or worse will the climate get, overall and in particular locations? What factors account for observed or inferred changes? What is the role of human factors? How much can humans intentionally affect climates, and should we? What are the tradeoffs of acting or not acting in particular ways to try to influence particular effects?

These questions are difficult and deeply contested among experts. But government officials often think otherwise. In April 2016, about 20 U.S. attorneys general announced the formation of "AGs United for Clean Power" in order to aggressively investigate and punish dissenters from their orthodoxy that "As we all know, global warming, if not reversed, will be catastrophic for our planet" (Schneiderman 2016). New York's attorney general added, "a lot of us ... in state government are prepared to step into this battle with an unprecedented level of commitment and coordination" (Exxon Mobil Corporation 2016).

One immediate result was a massive subpoena from the attorney general of the U.S. Virgin Islands, Claude Walker, against Exxon Mobil Corporation, intended to punish the company and chill the expression of dissent from his view that "[w]e cannot continue to rely on fossil fuel … We have to look at renewable energy. That's the only solution" (Exxon Mobil Corporation 2016).

The subpoena targeted not just the company but also dozens of professors and scientists, as the company describes in its lawsuit:

> The subpoena also appears to target individuals and entities that hold policy views with which Attorney General Walker disagrees. The subpoena requests "[a]ll Documents or Communications concerning research, advocacy, strategy, reports, studies, reviews, or public opinions regarding Climate Change sent to or received from" 88 named organizations, three-quarters of which have been identified by environmental advocacy groups as opposing policies in favor of addressing climate change or disputing the science in support of climate change. It requests similar documents and communications from 54 named scientists, professors, and other professionals.
>
> *(Exxon Mobil Corporation 2016)*

Six years earlier, the tables had been turned when Virginia's attorney general issued a civil investigative demand (CID) targeting climate scientist Michael Mann for possible fraud. In the CID, the office of Attorney General Kenneth T. Cuccinelli II commanded that the University of Virginia produce a huge swath of documents involving dozens upon dozens of scholars and other individuals in order to determine whether Mann violated the Virginia Fraud Against Taxpayers Act. The CID warned against "post normal" scientists who engage in activism and seem to lower their standards in order to make a better rhetorical case for their preferred policy. In particular, the CID argued that in seeking funds from Virginia, Mann relied on flawed scientific papers: "Some of the conclusions of the papers demonstrate a complete lack of rigor regarding the statistical analysis of the alleged data." To the extent that Mann should have known better, the CID argued, he was liable under the law (Russell 2010).

Climate science is, of course, not the only example. In 2009, conservative members of the Oklahoma legislature launched an investigation of the University of Oklahoma because it had tolerated atheist Richard Dawkins on campus. One legislator attempted to pass two bills condemning Dawkins and proclaiming evolution "unproven and unpopular" (Lukianoff 2009). This legislative bullying was in the tradition of Tennessee's Butler Act, which had banned universities and other schools from teaching human evolution, leading to the infamous 1925 case *The State of Tennessee v. John Thomas Scopes* and the founding of a private college, now known as Bryan College, to carry forth the state's official creationist views as held by William Jennings Bryan. Although Tennessee repealed the Butler Act in 1967, Bryan College demands that its faculty conform to an even stricter view of creationism today (Adams 2014).

Official government values and official government facts lead government officials to exert their power to rein in those with different values and different research findings. Demands that universities submit to fishing expeditions in order to enable civil or criminal investigations, putting unscientific enforcers in charge of evaluating all the utterances of dozens of professors over long periods of time, are recipes for massive abuse of government power. Ideology combined with massive power makes the government the prime threat to free and open inquiry.

The government's research agendas

The public funding of American higher education is far from neutral. The government's billions of dollars for higher education research and other education subsidies often come attached not to strings but to iron bars.

The National Science Foundation (NSF), for instance, funds science and engineering projects proposed by about 2,000 grantee organizations. It funds about 11,000 proposals out of 40,000 submitted each year (National Science Foundation 2016a). In 2009 the American Recovery and Reinvestment Act (ARRA) directed six billion dollars to academic institutions in addition to prior commitments, about half of it to NSF. This meant that "ARRA funding accounted for 16.2% of the $36.2 billion obligated to 1,447 academic institutions" (Yamaner 2009).

To be sure, NSF grants cover a wide variety of topics – even political science. Should political science research receive NSF funds? That is not a scientific question so much as a political one. It should come as no surprise, then, that the American Political Science Association (APSA) and its members lobby the U.S. Congress for money through direct action by scholars:

> APSA is a member of the Consortium of Social Science Associations (COSSA) and the Coalition for National Science Funding (CNSF). Each year, APSA participates in COSSA's Advocacy Day, which brings scholars to Capitol Hill to discuss the importance of political science research and express support for strong funding for the National Science Foundation.
>
> *(American Political Science Association 2016)*

This effort has been particularly important to APSA in light of efforts by now-retired U.S. Senator Tom Coburn of Oklahoma against NSF funding for such research. Senator Coburn's amendment to a 2009 appropriations bill would have eliminated this funding. A study by two University of Miami professors regarding senators' votes on the amendment found that "the number of top-tier political science Ph.D. programs in the senator's state," among other factors, significantly predicted the vote (Uscinski and Klofstad 2010).

Apart from political science, should NSF fund two additional sea-based research vessels or not? That's something members of Congress want to decide, too (Mervis 2016).

And should the director of NSF have an agenda? France Córdova does, and she revealed it in May 2016. Among her top interests is climate change in the Arctic (Idso, Carter, and Singer 2015). Córdova takes for granted "the unprecedented rate of Arctic environmental and social change" and states the following as fact:

> The Arctic is warming at twice the rate of the rest of the Earth, with far-reaching consequences for Arctic residents, particularly indigenous peoples. Arctic change will fundamentally alter climate, weather, and ecosystems globally in ways that we do not yet understand, but which will have profound impacts on the world's economy and security.
>
> *(National Science Foundation 2016b)*

The Arctic science is not as settled as the NSF director suggests (see, e.g., Lansner 2016). If you are a researcher who is not already on board with Córdova's facts and inferences, good luck with your NSF grant proposal. Any conception that government funding of academic research is "neutral" is deeply misconceived (see Engell and Dangerfield 2005: 213).

Let us imagine that McDonald's wanted to support academic research on the topic of sustainability. This is in fact a high priority for McDonald's, which intends to "make sustainability the new normal – for our business, society and the world at large" (McDonald's 2016). Whether McDonald's wants this result or the opposite, the funded science ought to be subject to the same standards as though it were funded by anyone else: a private research university, like Harvard with its official puritan values; a public research university beholden to the state like the University of Virginia, where the attorney general could threaten fraud charges; or the National Science Foundation, which controls literally billions of dollars and is beholden to the federal government.

Now, if a university fails to meet all of the standards enforced by the Department of Justice and the Department of Education – which include ideology-based speech restrictions – that university can lose all of its federal funding. Yale University, for instance, would lose about 500 million dollars per year (Foundation for Individual Rights in Education 2011). Universities that resist, such as Tufts University, are forced to bend the knee (Bader 2014). Only one university in the country, Oklahoma Wesleyan University, has sued the Department of Education for its ideological overreach, more than five years after it violated the Administrative Procedure Act in its ideological reinterpretation of nondiscrimination law (Kruth 2016). And all federal student loans now run through the Department of Education, which faces calls to distribute loan dollars according to government agendas (Kothari and Ray 2016). Which dollars are most likely to compromise free speech and academic freedom, and which dollars are most in danger of coercing academia? Not McDonald's dollars but government dollars.

Academic authorities

If scholars cannot trust ideological powers or state powers to safeguard academic freedom, and if McDonaldized campus administrators have strong incentives to violate freedom of expression in order to keep the peace on campus and avoid federal investigations, whom can they trust? Can they trust one another? With due respect to Winston Churchill's quip about democracy ([1947] 2011), one might observe that peer review is the worst form of academic accountability – except for all the other forms that have been tried from time to time.

Indeed, scholars are not immune to perverse incentives, and professional associations themselves often beset professors with ideological pressure. Since occupational licensing is enforced by the government, professional associations that restrict speech as a condition of licensure effectively employ the government's power to censor.

Kant observes that in medicine, for instance,

> the government watches over the public's convenience [and] safety ... And since these two services are the function of a police force, all medical regulations really have to do only with policing the medical profession. [Physicians] remain subject to the judgment of their faculty in matters which concern the medical police and so interest the government.
>
> *([1798] 1992: 41–43)*

Perhaps it is just that fraudulent claims of medical expertise that lead to patients' deaths are within the legitimate scope of government, yet the judge still must ask doctors to advise on what counts as sufficient medical expertise. Unelected practitioners thus effectively exercise a part of the police power.

The most recent example of this situation in the United States involves the policing of lawyers by the American Bar Association (ABA), which in August 2016 promulgated new rules prohibiting speech that "manifests bias." The rules are not saved by couching them in terms of ethics or "professional misconduct," for they express the ideological biases of the association's own rulegivers. Since the federal government has given the ABA the power to accredit law schools – and since accreditation is a requirement for federal subsidies – the ABA effectively makes its ideology a national requirement (Rotunda 2016; Volokh 2016).

The ideological policing of the helping professions in America provides many more examples. For instance, in 2012, Eastern Michigan University, a government university, won a lawsuit permitting it to require students to adhere to its politically biased code of ethics. This code mirrors the Code of Ethics of the American Counseling Association. In the name of nondiscrimination, the code demands that counselors betray their deeply held beliefs in order to provide counseling that enables people to persist in destructive behaviors, as seen from the perspective of some counselors. That is, if a counselor believes that a transgendered person suffers from a malady and should not be fully supported in one's disordered beliefs about oneself, the counselor is forced to support the patient anyway, within the bounds of the ACA's dictates, even though the counselor sees this practice as further harming the patient. The counselor is not permitted to simply refer the patient to a different counselor who intends to fully support the transgendered person's identity and beliefs (Rudow 2013).

Such scenarios also include the internal policing of faculty members' speech by one another, even at private universities. The Harvard faculty's firing of Professor Swamy is one example. More recently, Oberlin College, a private college in Ohio, announced that a professor who had made "anti-Semitic" statements on her personal Facebook page was suspended pending a review by her faculty peers. The faculty judges have been asked to judge her "professional fitness" (Flaherty 2016). And the most frequent internal policing of faculty research occurs through institutional review boards, which are mandated by federal law and which violate academic freedom in every case by forcing professors not to engage in any research involving people, and not to publish the results, until a censorship board (which often includes non-professors, besides faculty from far-flung departments) has approved everything about the research (Hamburger 2007).

Although bodies of experts cannot be trusted to uphold the freedoms of their own members, it does not seem to be a solution to put some other body, such as government regulators, in charge of the boundaries by which a profession polices itself. Ideology and nonacademic incentives are most dangerous in the hands of those who have the most power, that is, government regulators.

The following section presents a few proposals for preserving the Republic of Science despite having no one to trust.

Proposals to promote free and open inquiry

This chapter has shown that campus ideology, government power, and academic authorities all threaten free and open inquiry on campus. One might despair that the United States, despite its reputation for having the leading universities in the world, nevertheless fails so miserably, time after time, in preventing such threats from limiting the academic freedom of professors. Possible solutions must accept the reality that power will be abused.

To approach a solution, one might note that Americans have faced this kind of problem before. The metaphor of the Republic of Science provides insight. While the U.S. Constitution divides powers and forces them to be checked and balanced in the American republic, the Republic of Science may need just such a structure.

Government power is already limited by the First Amendment, which has been incorporated against the U.S. states and thus prevents public universities from punishing professors in violation of their rights. This limitation is far from sufficient. Government dollars massively distort higher education to conform to government agendas. Limiting these dollars and their attendant content and viewpoint pressures is an important route to diminishing this power.

Student loans, for instance, should be entirely privatized. In the light of calls to restrict aid based on government-favored outcomes, such as job preparation instead of liberal education, government ought to leave the scene. This abdication will enable colleges to choose their own curricula without fear that government officials will pressure them to change. In addition, most, if not all, funding for academic research ought to be privatized. Having a huge number of competing forces to choose from will provide scholars with maximum freedom to pursue the dollars and research that best fit their academic interests.

What proposals, in turn, provide checks against the abuses of power within a university? Ending the government imposition of institutional review boards – and ending them altogether – will help. Decentralization and clarification of the powers of shared governance also will help. Decentralization means that those who are closest to any academic decision should have the power to decide what to do with their own resources. Shared governance complicates the matter, since the same course, for instance, may be simultaneously within the purview of a professor, a department that has required it, and the whole college due to core curriculum requirements. Making it clear ahead of time which elements of the course are controlled by which power, a form of property rights in one's courses, will reduce conflict and abuse of power.

Colleges and universities that do not wish to operate as seminaries also ought to adopt a statement such as the University of Chicago's Kalven Committee Report, which pledges ideological neutrality at the level of the whole university. This statement is worth quoting at length, because it has kept the University of Chicago out of many a controversy and much mischief since it was adopted in 1967:

> A university has a great and unique role to play in fostering the development of social and political values in a society....
>
> Its domain of inquiry and scrutiny includes all aspects and all values of society. A university faithful to its mission will provide enduring challenges to social values, policies, practices, and institutions. By design and by effect, it is the institution which creates discontent with the existing social arrangements and proposes new ones. In brief, a good university, like Socrates, will be upsetting.
>
> The instrument of dissent and criticism is the individual faculty member or the individual student. The university is the home and sponsor of critics; it is not itself the critic. It is, to go back once again to the classic phrase, a community of scholars. To perform its mission in the society, a university must sustain an extraordinary environment of freedom of inquiry and maintain an independence from political fashions, passion, and pressures. A university, if it is to be true to its faith in intellectual inquiry, must embrace, be hospitable to, and encourage the widest diversity of views within its own community. It is a community but only for the limited, albeit great, purposes of teaching and research. It is not a club, it is not a trade association, it is not a lobby.
>
> Since the university is a community only for these limited and distinctive purposes, it is a community which cannot take collective action on the issues of the day without endangering the conditions for its existence and

effectiveness. There is no mechanism by which it can reach a collective position without inhibiting that full freedom of dissent on which it thrives. It cannot insist that all of its members favor a given view of social polity; if it takes collective action, therefore, it does so at the price of censuring any minority who do not agree with the view adopted. In brief, it is a community which cannot resort to majority vote to reach positions on public issues.

The neutrality of the university as an institution arises then not from a lack of courage nor out of indifference and insensitivity. It arises out of respect for free inquiry and the obligation to cherish a diversity of viewpoints. And this neutrality as an institution has its complement in the fullest freedom for its faculty and students as individuals to participate in political action and social protest....

Moreover, the sources of power of a great university should not be misconceived. Its prestige and influence are based on integrity and intellectual competence; they are not based on the circumstance that it may be wealthy, may have political contacts, and may have influential friends.

(Kalven 1967)

The Kalven Committee Report functions similarly to the First Amendment. That is, it is a voluntary limitation on the official power of the university, clearing the way for professors and academic units to teach and to pursue wisdom and truth with broad academic freedom.

Finally, to limit the abuse of power by professional associations, no one body should be the monopolistic gatekeeper of the ethics of a profession. Occupational licensing should be abolished or, failing that, opened up to a diverse group of licensers that have minimal or zero oversight by government ideologues. Universities, in turn, should beware of limiting curriculum to fit the licensure requirements of a monopolistic actor such as, in law, a state bar.

Conclusion

The more colleges and universities function like a constitutional republic, the more likely they are to preserve free and open inquiry. The forces of ideology, state, and professional associations are very strong, but they can be counteracted through institutional arrangements that set power against power. Furthermore, limiting the influence of the largest threat to academic freedom – government dollars – will free universities to make their own way in the marketplace of ideas.

References

Adams, M. (2014) The King of Bryan College, 29 July: http://townhall.com/columnists/m ikeadams/2014/07/29/the-king-of-bryan-college-n1870820 (accessed 23 August 2016).
American Political Science Association (2016) National Science Foundation, http://www. apsanet.org/advocacy/nsf (accessed 23 August 2016).

Augustine of Hippo ([397] 1996) *De Doctrina Christiana (Oxford Early Christian Texts)*, edited and translated by Green, R.P.H., Oxford: Clarendon Press.

Bader, H. (2014) Punishment First, Trial Later, or Never: The Education Department's Investigation of Tufts University, Competitive Enterprise Institute, 21 May: https://cei.org/blog/punishment-first-trial-later-or-never-education-departments-investigation-tufts-university?page=1 (accessed 23 August 2016).

Churchill, W. ([1947] 2011) House of Commons speech, November 11, 1947, in Richard Langworth, ed., *Churchill by Himself: The Definitive Collection of Quotations*, New York: Public Affairs: 574.

Cohn, J. (2014) South Carolina Budget Punishes Colleges for LGBT Books, Violates Academic Freedom, Foundation for Individual Rights in Education, 13 June: https://www.thefire.org/south-carolina-budget-punishes-colleges-for-lgbt-books-violates-academic-freedom/ (accessed 23 August 2016).

Cohn, J. (2016) Tennessee Bill to Punish UT for Sex Week Becomes Law, Foundation for Individual Rights in Education, 23 May: https://www.thefire.org/tennessee-bill-to-punish-ut-for-sex-week-becomes-law/ (accessed 23 August 2016).

Creeley, W. (2014) A Year Later, Impact of Feds' 'Blueprint' Comes into Focus, Foundation for Individual Rights in Education, 28 August: https://www.thefire.org/year-later-impact-feds-blueprint-comes-focus/ (accessed 23 August 2016).

Engell, J. and Dangerfield, A. (2005) *Saving Higher Education in the Age of Money*, Charlottesville: University of Virginia Press.

Ethics & Religious Liberty Commission (2016) Protecting the Future of Religious Higher Education, 9 August: http://erlc.com/resource-library/statements/protecting-the-future-of-religious-higher-education (accessed 23 August 2016).

Exxon Mobil Corporation v. Claude Earl Walker (2016) Case no. 017-284890-16, Tarrant County, Texas: https://cei.org/sites/default/files/Exxon%20petition%20April%2013%202016.pdf (accessed 23 August 2016).

Flaherty, C. (2016) Suspended for Anti-Semitism, *Inside Higher Ed*, 4 August: https://www.insidehighered.com/news/2016/08/04/months-later-oberlin-suspends-professor-who-made-anti-semitic-remarks-facebook (accessed 23 August 2016).

Foundation for Individual Rights in Education (2011) Frequently Asked Questions: OCR's April 4 'Dear Colleague' Guidance Letter, 15 August: https://www.thefire.org/frequently-asked-questions-ocrs-april-4-dear-colleague-guidance-letter/ (accessed 23 August 2016).

Foundation for Individual Rights in Education (2016) Harvard University: Blacklisting of Final Club, Fraternity, and Sorority Students: https://www.thefire.org/cases/harvard-university-blacklisting-of-final-club-fraternity-and-sorority-students/ (accessed 23 August 2016).

Hasson, P. (2016) D.C. Will Fine You for Calling a Transgender Person the 'Wrong' Pro-nouns, *Daily Caller*, 27 June: http://dailycaller.com/2016/06/27/d-c-will-fine-you-for-calling-a-transgender-person-the-wrong-pronouns/ (accessed 23 August 2016).

Hamburger, P. (2007). Getting Permission, *Northwestern University Law Review*, 101(2): 405–492.

Holmes, O. W. (1919) Abrams v. United States, dissent, 250 US 616.

Hume, D. ([1742] 1987) Of the Rise and Progress of the Arts and Sciences, in E. F. Miller, ed., *Essays, Moral, Political, and Literary*, Indianapolis, IN: Liberty Fund, Inc.: http://www.econlib.org/library/LFBooks/Hume/hmMPL14.html (accessed 23 August 2016).

Idso, C. D., Carter, R. M., and Singer, S. F. (2015) *Why Scientists Disagree about Global Warming*, Arlington Heights, IL: Heartland Institute.

Kalven, H., Jr. (1967). Kalven Committee: Report on the University's Role in Political and Social Action, 11 November: http://www-news.uchicago.edu/releases/07/pdf/kalverpt.pdf (accessed 23 August 2016).

Kant, I. ([1798] 1992) *The Conflict of the Faculties*, translated by Gregor, M. J., Lincoln, NE: University of Nebraska Press.

Kipnis, L. (2015a) Sexual Paranoia Strikes Academe, *Chronicle of Higher Education*, 27 February: http://laurakipnis.com/wp-content/uploads/2010/08/Sexual-Paranoia-Strikes-Academe.pdf (accessed 23 August 2016).

Kipnis, L. (2015b) My Title IX Inquisition, *Chronicle of Higher Education*, 29 May: http://laurakipnis.com/wp-content/uploads/2010/08/My-Title-IX-Inquisition-The-Chronicle-Review-.pdf (accessed 23 August 2016).

Kothari, S. P., and Ray, K. (2016) Bigger Loans for STEM Students, *Wall Street Journal*, 15 August: http://www.wsj.com/articles/bigger-loans-for-stem-students-1471210878 (accessed 23 August 2016).

Kruth, S. (2016) Oklahoma Wesleyan Joins Lawsuit Challenging 2011 'Dear Colleague' Letter, Foundation for Individual Rights in Education, 15 August: https://www.thefire.org/oklahoma-wesleyan-joins-lawsuit-challenging-2011-dear-colleague-letter/ (accessed 23 August 2016).

Lansner, F. (2016) Interesting and Positive Changes in Arctic Sea Ice Volume, 9 August: https://wattsupwiththat.com/2016/08/09/interesting-and-positive-changes-in-arctic-sea-ice-volume/comment-page-1/ (accessed 23 August 2016).

Lukianoff, G. (2009) Engaging the Oklahoma Legislature on Its Decision to Investigate Richard Dawkins' Free Speech, 20 May: https://www.thefire.org/engaging-the-oklahoma-legislature-on-its-decision-to-investigate-richard-dawkins-free-speech/ (accessed 23 August 2016).

Lukianoff, G. (2014) *Unlearning Liberty: Campus Censorship and the End of American Debate*, New York: Encounter Books.

Lukianoff, G., and Haidt, J. (2015) The Coddling of the American Mind, *The Atlantic*, September: http://www.theatlantic.com/magazine/archive/2015/09/the-coddling-of-the-american-mind/399356/ (accessed 23 August 2016).

McDonald's (2016) Sustainability: http://www.aboutmcdonalds.com/content/mcd/sustainability.html (accessed 23 August 2016).

Mervis, J. (2016) House Panel Would Block NSF from Building Two New Ships, *Science*, 19 May: http://www.sciencemag.org/news/2016/05/house-panel-would-block-nsf-building-two-new-ships (accessed 23 August 2016).

Mill, J. S. ([1859] 1879) *On Liberty and The Subjection of Women*, New York: Henry Holt: http://oll.libertyfund.org/titles/347 (accessed 23 August 2016).

Milton, J. ([1644] 1918) Areopagitica with a Commentary by Sir Richard C. Jebb and with Supplementary Material, Cambridge at the University Press: http://oll.libertyfund.org/titles/103 (accessed 23 August 2016).

National Science Foundation (2016a) About Funding: http://www.nsf.gov/funding/aboutfunding.jsp (accessed 23 August 2016).

National Science Foundation (2016b) NSF Ideas for Future Investment, 2 May: http://www.sciencemag.org/sites/default/files/documents/Big%20Ideas%20compiled.pdf (accessed 23 August 2016).

Polanyi, M. (1962) The Republic of Science: Its Political and Economic Theory, *Minerva*, (1): 54–74: http://sciencepolicy.colorado.edu/students/envs_5100/polanyi_1967.pdf (accessed 19 August 2016).

Rauch, J. ([1995] 2013) *Kindly Inquisitors: The New Attacks on Free Thought*, Expanded Edition, Chicago: University of Chicago Press.

Rotunda, R. (2016) The ABA Overrules the First Amendment, *Wall Street Journal*, 16 August: http://www.wsj.com/articles/the-aba-overrules-the-first-amendment-1471388418 (accessed 23 August 2016).

Rudow, H. (2013) Resolution of EMU Case Confirms ACA Code of Ethics, Counseling Profession's Stance against Client Discrimination, 9 January: http://ct.counseling.org/2013/01/resolution-of-emu-case-confirms-aca-code-of-ethics-counseling-professions-stance-against-client-discrimination/ (accessed 23 August 2016).

Russell, W. G., Jr. (2010) Civil Investigative Demand No. 3-MM, 29 September, Office of the Attorney General, Commonwealth of Virginia, Richmond, VA: http://voices.washingtonpost.com/virginiapolitics/New%20Mann%20CID.PDF (accessed 23 August 2016).

Schneiderman, E. (2016) A. G. Schneiderman, Former Vice President Al Gore and a Coalition of Attorneys General from across the Country Announce Historic State-Based Effort to Combat Climate Change, 29 March: http://www.ag.ny.gov/press-release/ag-schneiderman-former-vice-president-al-gore-and-coalition-attorneys-general-across (accessed 23 August 2016).

Silverglate, H. (2013) The Slow Death of Free Speech at Harvard, speech to the 55th reunion of the Harvard Law School class of 1958, Foundation for Individual Rights in Education, October 26: https://www.thefire.org/the-slow-death-of-free-speech-at-harvard (accessed 23 August 2016).

Uscinski, J. E., and Klofstad, C. A. (2010) Who Likes Political Science? Determinants of Senators' Votes on the Coburn Amendment, *Political Science and Politics*, 43(4): 701–706: http://www.as.miami.edu/personal/cklofstad/10_coburn.pdf (accessed 23 August 2016).

Volokh, E. (2016) A Speech Code for Lawyers, Banning Viewpoints That Express 'Bias,' Including in Law-Related Social Activities, *Washington Post*, 10 August: https://www.washingtonpost.com/news/volokh-conspiracy/wp/2016/08/10/a-speech-code-for-lawyers-banning-viewpoints-that-express-bias-including-in-law-related-social-activities-2 (accessed 23 August 2016).

Wells, H. G. (1918) *Joan and Peter: The Story of an Education*, New York: Macmillan Co.

Williams, G. H. (2014) *Divinings: Religion at Harvard: From Its Origins in New England Ecclesiastical History to the 175th Anniversary of The Harvard Divinity School, 1636 – 1992*, Bristol, CT: Vandenhoeck & Ruprecht.

Yamaner, M. (2009) ARRA Provided $5.9 Billion in Federal Science and Engineering Obligations to Universities and Colleges in FY 2009, June: http://www.nsf.gov/statistics/infbrief/nsf12320/ (accessed 23 August 2016).

7

BEYOND MCTHINKING

James Panton

I believe that the primary purpose of A Levels is to prepare students for degree-level study. All students should have access to qualifications that are highly respected and valued by leading universities. Current A Levels do not always provide the solid foundation that students need to prepare them for degree-level study and for vocational education. The modular nature of the qualifications and repeated assessment windows have contributed to many students not developing deep understanding or the necessary skills to make connections between topics. Many leading universities are concerned about current A Levels, and nearly three-quarters of lecturers say that they have had to adapt their teaching approaches for underprepared first year undergraduates.

Rt. Hon. Michael Gove MP, Secretary of State for Education, 22 January 2013

The transformation of UK universities from elite institutions serving a tiny proportion of the population into mass institutions serving an ever-expanding majority of school levers – not to mention post-school returners and 'life-long learners' – has raised many questions for those of us involved in education in the 21st century. Inevitably, there are questions about the putative purpose of higher education, about the content of courses and the intellectual standards required of students setting out on their university career. If Michael Gove is right that the primary purpose of A Levels is to prepare students for university, for those of us involved in sixth form education, there are important questions to be asked about the extent to which the content of and approach we take to sixth form education can prepare an increasing majority of students for higher level university study.

In order to give some definition to these latter questions we should first be aware of just how significant an increase there has been in the number of sixth formers aspiring to, and successfully gaining entry into, university. A decade before Michael Gove began his A Level shake-up in 2013, a previous Education Secretary, Charles Clarke, addressed the House of Commons to clarify his government's commitment to 'increase participation in higher education towards 50 per cent of young people between 18 and 30 by the end of the decade' (Clark 2003). This stated commitment that half of all young people would go to university followed on from what had already been a remarkable period of university expansion. In 1950, participation rates in higher education in the UK were around 3 per cent. Twenty years later, they were 8.4 per cent, and by 1990, they had risen to 19 per cent. By 2000, this rate was at 33 per cent (Bolton 2012). To put those increases into stark relief: in the thirteen years between 1989 and 2002, university student numbers rose by an incredible 94 per cent (Brown 2003: 3). Although more than a decade after Clarke's address the 50 per cent target has yet to be achieved, in 2013 there were jubilant reports that we were 'nearly there' when the Department of Business, Innovation and Skills announced a Higher Education Initial Participation Rate (HEIPR) of 49 per cent in 2013 (DBIS 2013). This does not mean nearly half of the 18-year-olds leaving school in the UK went to university in 2013. Rather, the calculation takes a broad definition of higher education that includes everything from foundation degrees at FE Colleges to post-graduate research degrees at Oxbridge and is based upon sampling 17–30-year-olds, who are attending university in the UK for the first time (see Ball 2013). A more realistic assessment of the numbers of school leavers going directly into university is given by the *Times Higher Education* 'World University Rankings', which puts the figure at around 30 per cent of English 18-year-olds gaining a university place through the University and College Admissions Service (UCAS) in the autumn of 2015 (Dorling 2015). That is still a remarkable proportion of school leavers. Around half a million people took up a place at university last year.

For some, the 50 per cent policy target was always a fool's errand. 'Labour's target of getting 50 per cent of young people to go to university has driven down standards and devalued degrees' was the stated conclusion of a report by The Association of Graduate Recruiters in 2010 (Williams 2010). The substantive criticism of the target is that radically expanding access to university without fundamentally shaking up the pre-university education system could not but result in the degeneration of standards in higher education. The target appeared little more than a catchy sound bite that somehow was transformed into a government policy. Personally, I welcome the idea of opening the transformative experience that a rigorous higher education can provide to as many school-leavers who aspire to the intellectual challenge. However, I am sympathetic to the criticism that, in our current climate we have failed to raise the educational bar for enough students in pre-university education. It is not clear to me that sufficient young people are intellectually equipped for the challenge that a properly 'higher' education should set them. Whether or not a majority of them could, or should be, and whether or not there are a sufficient number of 'degree' courses, which, at present, set that challenge well enough, are questions I will leave for others to address. Here I wish to focus on a slightly different set of priorities around the teaching of students at sixth form level.

★★★

As teachers at A Level, our task is to take students on a journey that challenges them intellectually, that cultivates curiosity and excitement for the disciplines we are ourselves excited and curious about. The aim is to take them through a transition between learning facts and properly knowing information to really beginning to understand the composition of a discipline. There are still facts that must be learned and syllabi that must be followed, but students at A Level should also begin to deepen their understanding by developing the capacity to read and think more critically, and perhaps more originally. In their final two years of secondary level education, a time that until recently could still be called post-compulsory education, our task is to open students' minds, expand horizons, deepen knowledge, encourage autonomy, and in sum, to deliver an intellectually transformative experience.

One obvious problem for those of us in the teaching profession is how to tell when we are doing a good job.

In a reversal of Hegel's famous dictum in the *Science of Logic* that at a certain developmental stage all *quantitative* change becomes *qualitative*, the education system we work in, which is itself part of a remarkably instrumentalized culture, demands that all quality must find its expression in quantitative terms. The measure of good teaching is thus primarily measurable by the results achieved by students in exams. An increasingly significant criterion against which individual teachers and schools as a whole are judged is the proportion of their charges that achieve the results in examination that meet or better their university offers. It is not wrong, although it may be sometimes limiting, that as an A Level teacher I should measure my worth against my capacity to help students achieve results that will allow them to embark on university courses they are excited to take up.

There is a problematic tension for educators, however. We want to provide an education for young people that can be a transformative intellectual experience. We also want, and need, to teach our students to gain the highest possible marks in examinations. As far as these twin wants coincide, we can be sure we are doing a good job as educators and working in an examination system that is setting the right criteria by which life-changing academic judgements are made about our students. However, it is not clear that the desire to educate and the desire to achieve top marks in exams have consistently coincided in recent years.

One obvious area for concern over a number of years is the tendency for more and more students to achieve the top results. In 1982, only 62 per cent of students sitting A Levels in England achieved a pass mark; by 2011, the pass rate had reached 97.8 per cent (Hartford 2012). From the 1950s, when A Levels were first introduced, until the mid-1980s, the proportion of A Level entries achieving an A-grade result sat at under 10 per cent. In 1980, achieving an A grade would put students in the top 8 per cent of examinees. By 1990 that figure was 12 per cent; by 2000 it had reached 17 per cent, and by 2010, 27 per cent (see Coughlan 2014). The continuous rise in the numbers of student achieving the top grade at A Level led inevitably to questions about the reliability of A grades as a marker of excellence. Rather than recalibrate the marks, with the consequence that fewer students would achieve at the top level, a more short-term instrumental solution was adopted by introducing an A★ grade in summer 2010. The rationale for this new highest level grade was 'to help higher education institutions to differentiate between the highest achieving candidates applying to the most oversubscribed courses and to promote and reward greater stretch and challenge' (Nadir and Carmen 2014). An old fashioned A grade no longer marks out high achievement. In August 2014, the first time that the proportion of A grades at A Level fell (slightly!) in over 30 years, 26 per cent of exam entries achieved an A grade, of which 8 per cent achieved the newer A★ (Coughlan 2014).

This ever-greater 'improvement' in results could be explained by on-going improvements in the quality of teaching provision. It is certainly the case that the teaching profession has become increasingly 'professionalized' – with a far greater emphasis upon the presentation and packaging of exam syllabi and preparing students to sit examinations. Moreover, A Levels are not the only arena in which exam results have improved. Between 2002 and 2011 the number of first-class degree results awarded by UK universities more than doubled, from 26,100 to 53,215. Maybe young people are just more intelligent than they used to be? More likely, however, is that the meaning of the awards themselves has been gradually but consistently eroded. As one academic and critic of grade inflation put it: 'Everybody gets a first or a 2:1 ... a 2:2 is the new fail' (Hadfield 2014).

We need to understand that grade inflation is a complicated process. It is not merely a loss of nerve amongst examiners who begin to award higher grades for poorer quality work. Rather, the organization of both the content and delivery of academic disciplines has become increasingly oriented towards enabling increasing numbers of students to achieve better and better grades. For a number of years courses have been divided into 'modularized' component parts, meaning the students can be taught very specific chunks of knowledge and information oriented towards regular examinations that provide component parts of the overall result. There has also been a tendency for students to sit and then resit exams in order to maximize marks, meaning that each individual exam result comes to have a provisional character.

The tendency towards modularity across the system as a whole is reflected in the internal organization of exams themselves, which tend to break substantive questions down into chunks which are organized in such a way as to build difficulty and depth up through the component parts of the answer to the question. Thus a question will be divided into part (a) which will award marks for factual recall, part (b) which will be lots of factual recall with a bit of analysis, and part (c) which will contain a requirement for factual recall, analysis and something that is beginning to look like an argument. The rationale for breaking questions down into more manageable chunks is that weaker students will be able to prove skills in earlier parts of their answer, and thus not be so heavily discriminated against; and all students will become more able to recognize the different component parts of evidence, analysis, structure and argument in the presentation of their ideas and arguments. However, there are very obvious problems. The first is that in seeking to find recognition for weaker students we lose the scope to stretch all students. The second problem is that students need to be very carefully taught how to approach these exams in terms of what kinds of answers are needed for which bits of a question, and how to achieve top marks in each section. The focus of teaching moves from disciplinary content to the complexities of an exam specification.

This restructuring of the system of examining student achievement has thus driven a quite fundamental reorientation of the process of teaching subject knowledge itself. Rather than exams being a test of knowledge and ability that we bolt on at the end of a long period of intellectual study and enrichment, we have, over a number of years, come to orient and subordinate the qualitative intellectual process of teaching and learning towards the quantitative outcome: marks achieved on an exam paper. When I first entered the teaching profession I was shocked to discover the extent to which my ambitious students would know that they had to study the Mark Schemes and Examiners' Reports published by exam boards from very early on in the course because they wanted to have a clear understanding of how to achieve marks in the exams. A substantial part of my classroom activity is spent directly preparing students for the complexities of the exam: clarifying what needs to be said where, how many points need to be made using what kinds of examples. So while subject knowledge is still necessary, the student has come to understand the subject as a series of discrete component parts that must be added together to create an exam answer. It is entirely possible to achieve full marks in exams precisely because the achievement of marks is determined by the students' capacity to meet the requirements set out on a Mark Scheme which examiners will use to grade their answers.

If our task as educators is to help students get the best possible marks in exams, the system works. It is entirely possible to get weaker students better grades by focussing upon chunks of content and the mastery of exam board 'Assessment Objectives'. Whether or not this kind of focus can be equally successful in transforming weaker students into stronger students with a deeper understanding of the discipline and a greater ability to pursue and further develop their own understanding, is less clear. There is also lots of anecdotal evidence from colleagues in different subjects around the country that there is a tendency for the brightest students with the greatest propensity for originality and critical insight to do less well than we might expect in exams because they produce answers that fall beyond the quite tight remit of the examiners' marking scheme. The solution here is to drill all students well to ensure that they will only produce the kinds of answers the examiners are expecting.

Of course, the best and most enthusiastic teachers will find ways of pushing and stretching their students intellectually. There is a lot to be said in favour of giving students a very clear sense of how to achieve the best possible results. The problem is that the achievement of results becomes an increasingly technical process within which subject is organized around exam criteria. When the measure of good teaching is in large part determined by the success of students in exams there are very great incentives for teachers to spend a large proportion of their time preparing students for exams as a process, which has become increasingly elided with teaching students the rigours and foundations of a discipline.

★★★

In 2013 then-Secretary of State for Education, Michael Gove, sent a letter to Glenys Stacey, the then-Chief Executive of the Office of Qualifications and Examinations Regulation (Ofqual), setting out a range of concerns about the current state of A Level examinations (Gove 2013). Principal among these concerns was the idea that A Levels were not giving a rigorous enough foundation in the disciplines they purported to be presenting, and that universities had become concerned that A Levels were failing to equip many students properly for higher level study. The result has been a quite radical shake-up of A Levels which is (at time of writing) still underway.

One priority has been to move away from modularized assessment structures composed of composite bite-sized chunks with the opportunity for regular resits towards a more traditional one- or two-year course with end-of-course examinations taken all at one time, and with less opportunity to resit. The distinction between AS (Advanced Supplementary) and A Level, which was introduced in 1989 to broaden the number of subjects students could study, remains; however, it is no longer the case that AS Levels will count towards overall A Level results. Students will either sit an AS Level or an A Level, where the latter will be recognized as a higher level qualification. This means for many students applying to university far more will depend (at least in theory) upon their performance in exams sat after two years of study.

A second priority has been to involve university academics and subject specialists far more in the process of determining both the disciplinary content and the 'skills' developed through the syllabi and tested in the exams (see Ofqual 2015).

Ofqual has set a timetable for the content reform of all A Level subjects. The first of these newly reformed subjects have been taught since September 2015, and students sitting AS Level exams in those subjects will have done so in July 2016. Students sitting A Levels in those subjects will not sit them until July 2017. The last of the subjects to reform will be first taught from September 2017 and first examined in July 2018 (AS) and 2019 (A Level). It is therefore too early to make any reliable judgement upon what the real outcome of these reforms will be. At time of writing, we remain a full month away from the first set of exam results. However, there are a number of reflections that it is possible to give on this process of reform and its likely consequences.

The ambition and motivation for these quite radical reforms is good, in my view. Any attempt to shake up the structure of education will always be met by resistance from teachers, but the need to rethink what we are doing at school level, and to open upon new possibilities to experiment, has never been greater. The attempt to make sixth form level subjects more academically rigorous, and to move away from the tendency to teach towards the test, which has become so dominant in the secondary school sector, is a bold but necessary step. Moving away from modularized teaching and assessment by opening up the possibility for teachers to work with students over the course of two years before they are formally examined opens up the exciting possibility of really engaging with students in the development of deep subject knowledge and disciplinary learning. Exams at the end of two years give students the possibility to grow and mature intellectually through the study of a discipline and thus raise the possibility of results being a far more rigorous and fairer test of their ability at a subject.

However, as with many political reforms across a host of social policy areas, it is far from clear that the full organizational implications of these reforms have been properly thought through. Reforming A Levels in order to make them a better preparation for students applying to university is a good idea, but there are organizational problems that may yet undermine the ambition. At the moment, the many thousands of students who apply to university from sixth form do so with a range of AS Level results already in place. In the new system, the vast majority of those students will apply to university without any evidence of their performance in public examinations since their GCSEs. Many independent schools are already beginning to think about introducing their own systems of accountable and reliable internal examinations in order that their students can apply to university with some AS Level equivalent evidence of their ability. The ambition of making a clearer distinction between a long period of study and examinations at the end of that study may yet fail if there is no more fundamental reform to the process of university applications.

A second concern is that the redrafting of the content of subject syllabi under the close eye and, in some cases, quite explicit direction, of government ministers, may leave disciplines playing second fiddle to shorter term political priorities. After Ofqual draws up and consults on an overall specification for a subject, individual exam boards then put together more explicit proposals for how that content should be delivered and examined and how they will provide related teaching materials, resources and text books to accompany their version of the course. In my own primary subject, Government and Politics, after outcry from academic feminists that 'Feminism' would no longer be on the A2 syllabus (where it was, in fact, originally an optional component) the Government proposals have been hastily redrawn to include more discussion of feminism itself, and of gender equality, and to include more important women thinkers (see Grierson 2015 and Press Association 2016). There is no reason, in my mind, why such an important ideology should not be included. Nonetheless, along the way it would appear from current draft specifications that the Judiciary has lost its position as a distinct Branch of Government and the hugely influential American feminist and campaigner Betty Friedan has been included as an exponent of 'Liberalism' rather than 'Feminism'. There may well be too many cooks with too many different tastes and not nearly enough culinary skill involved in this process.

★★★

So how well do A Levels prepare students for university? This may well not be the right question to ask. At the moment A Levels sit within a culture in which education is understood in predominantly intsrumentalist terms: it is a means towards an end. In that culture it is inevitable the ends sought become the primary determinant of the content of education, and the principal measure of the quality and success of education. Hence, teachers are encouraged away from focussing upon subject knowledge, which becomes a secondary means towards the achievement of marks in examinations, and towards teaching students towards the exam. And indeed, the purpose of education at sixth form level is itself subordinated entirely towards the end of getting as many students as possible into university.

The problems which the currently in-process A Level reforms seek to address are deep and intertwined with an even deeper level malaise in which there is very little confidence institutionally in the value of what we do as teachers and educators. These problems cannot be quickly fixed with new specifications or short-term policies. This is not a reason to reject reform. On the contrary, much of the currently in-process A Level reform might yet bring some significant improvements. However, it is a reason to recognize the depth of the task we have before us.

References

Ball, C. (2013) Most people in the UK do not go to university – and maybe never will, *Guardian*, 4 June: https://www.theguardian.com/higher-education-network/blog/2013/jun/04/higher-education-participation-data-analysis (accessed 19 August 2016).

Bolton, P. (2012) *Education: Historical Statistics*. Standard Note: SN/SG/4252, 27 November. London: House of Commons Library.

Brown, N. (2003) What's it worth: the case for variable graduate contributions, A report for Universities UK.

Clark, C. (2003) Statement to the House of Commons, *Hansard*, 22 January, Column 303: http://www.publications.parliament.uk/pa/cm200203/cmhansrd/vo030122/debtext/30122-04.htm (accessed 19 August 2016).

Coughlan, S. (2014) A Level grades edge down, as university places rise, *BBC News*, 14 August: http://www.bbc.co.uk/news/education-28772974 (accessed 14 April 2016).

DBIS (2013) Participation rates in higher education: academic years 2006/2007–2011/2012 (Provisional), Department of Business, Innovation and Skills 'Statistical First Release', 24 April, London: DBIS.

Dorling, D. (2015) Six trends in university admissions, *Times Higher Education*, 12 February: https://www.timeshighereducation.com/features/danny-dorling-six-trends-in-university-admissions/2018407.article (accessed 19 August 2016).

Gove, M. (2013) Letter to Glenys Stacey, chief executive, Office of Qualifications and Examinations Regulation, 22 January: https://www.gov.uk/government/publications/letter-from-the-secretary-of-state-for-education-to-glenys-stacey-at-ofqual (accessed 19 August 2016).

Grierson, J. (2015) Plan to axe feminism from A-level politics triggers protest, *Guardian*, 20 November: https://www.theguardian.com/world/2015/nov/20/feminism-axed-a-level-politics-dfe-draft-protest (accessed 14 April 2016).

Hadfield, A. (2014) Degree classes mean nothing any more – let's ditch them, *Telegraph*, 5 July: http://www.telegraph.co.uk/education/universityeducation/10946514/Degree-classes-mean-nothing-any-more-lets-ditch-them.html (accessed 14 April 2016).

Hartford, J. (2012) We don't need no grade inflation, spiked, 4 April: http://www.spiked-online.com/newsite/article/12313#.V7rkDJgrLIU (accessed 14 April 2016).

Nadir, Z. and Carmen, V. R. (2014) The role of the A★ grade at A-level as a predictor of university performance, The Society for Research into Higher Education Conference: https://www.srhe.ac.uk/conference2014/abstracts/0083.pdf (accessed 14 April 2016).

Ofqual (2015) Get the facts: AS and A Level reform, 15 December: https://www.gov.uk/government/publications/get-the-facts-gcse-and-a-level-reform/get-the-facts-as-and-a-level-reform (accessed 14 April 2016).

Press Association (2016) Feminism to be reinstated to A-level politics syllabus, says schools minister, *Guardian*, 11 January: https://www.theguardian.com/education/2016/jan/11/feminism-reinstated-a-level-politics-syllabus-schools-minister (accessed 19 August 2016).

Williams, R. (2010) Abolish labour target of sending 50 percent to university, report urges, *Guardian*, 9 March: https://www.theguardian.com/education/2010/mar/09/abolish-50 percent-target (accessed 19 August 2016).

8

BEYOND 'STUDENT EXPERIENCE'

Ruth Mieschbuehler

The term 'student experience' can be found everywhere in university publicity material and on university web sites. The claim to offer an excellent 'student experience' is now seen as a selling point with which to convince student 'customers' to come through the door or through the gate and into the quad. Universities compete among themselves to be listed in league tables as the 'best' for student experience or even to be labelled as offering the 'most improved student experience'. University managers are now beginning to talk about university being made up of the 'student experience' and the 'academic experience' but that bifurcation plays down the changes brought about in the name of the 'student experience' across the university and in the academic disciplines.

The concept of the 'student experience' is very familiar but also very new (see Haselgrove 1994). It refers to a fundamental change in the university sector that has seen a growing rise in student-centred and learning-process-oriented teaching and a retreat from the academic disciplines that had its origins in the climate of change at the end of the last century. This was a time when – after the fall of the Berlin Wall in 1989 and the end of the Cold War – politics and attitudes to young people were changing. These changes can be summarized in the celebratory Western capitalist mantra, 'There is no alternative' (TINA). The consequences of TINA for young people was the rise of a new politics that saw them not as active agents for change but as vulnerable and in need of therapy (see Ecclestone and Hayes 2008: Chapter 7). This new socio-political attitude to young people is the explanation for the growing concern with the 'experience' of students.

The shift to the 'student experience' can be formally said to have taken hold in British higher education with the publication of the *Report of the National Committee of Inquiry into Higher Education* in 1997 (Dearing 1997). Since then, the rapid rise of the idea has led to a situation where university policies and practices, and university education, are rewritten and developed to meet the 'student experience' requirements. This fundamental change occurred at the same time as the mass expansion of higher education to cater for more and more young people. This 'massification' of higher education (Fox 2002) occurred at a time when going to university replaced getting a job and, ironically, when there was a loss of faith in knowledge, described by some as a 'fear of knowledge' (Boghossian 2007; Williams 2016). This is the historical context in which this unique concept of the 'student experience' arose and developed to become the guiding idea of the university in the twenty-first century.

It is important to be clear at the outset about what the 'student experience' is. The public relations hype masks this by celebrating any and every aspect of going to university. There are just three essential elements to the 'student experience' in universities. First, the adoption of 'student-centred' approaches to teaching and learning; second, the elevation of personal or cultural *experiences* over knowledge; third, the existence of a large institutional administration which supports that experience. The 'student experience' is not about ensuring students have a nice time – they can still organize that student experience for themselves – it is about the reorientation of academia around subjective experience rather than the pursuit of knowledge and understanding.

After almost two decades of endeavours aimed at meeting the requirements of the 'student experience', the effects on university education and academic life are clearly visible. There are many 'improvements' in provision external to the pursuit of knowledge – such as 'induction events', the provision of 'social learning spaces' and 'personal tutors' – which have been devised to enhance student satisfaction. In the classroom the 'student experience' manifests itself through an expansion of student-centred education, which shifts the focus of instruction from subject knowledge to motivational teaching techniques and curriculum content that is relevant to the life experience of students. Teaching has also become learning-process-oriented and distracts students from seeking subject knowledge by focusing their attention on 'learning how to learn'.

The effects on university education are devastating because universities are more concerned about student satisfaction, employability, the provision of modern facilities and comprehensive student support services and less about the pursuit of knowledge. A few simple steps to move beyond the 'student experience' are identified in this chapter. If these steps are not taken, universities will continue to reject knowledge-based education and the idea that the purpose of the university is the pursuit of knowledge.

The shift towards student-centred education

Recommendation eight of the *Report of the National Committee of Inquiry into Higher Education* entreated 'all institutions of higher education [to] give priority to developing and implementing learning and teaching strategies which focus on the promotion of students' learning' (Dearing 1997). This recommendation was readily implemented by universities already moving away from old-fashioned knowledge-based education towards student-centred education and learning-process-oriented teaching. After Dearing it was not long before the 'student experience' became integral to university policies and practice.

One way the new 'student experience' manifests itself is through the rising concern with student satisfaction. It is increasingly common to describe students as 'customers', and universities have entered a customer-service relationship with their students, which is why universities are concerned about student satisfaction (Woodall, Hiller and Resnick 2014). The current concern with the 'student journey' is believed to be essential to ensure 'student satisfaction'. The student journey starts with the application phase and the careful structuring of the interactions between potential students and the institution prior to arrival (Temple, Callender, Grove and Kersh 2014). The focus is then directed at the academic and campus experience and finally at the graduation phase and transition into employment (Temple *et al.* 2014). At each stage of the 'journey' student satisfaction is being assessed and policies and practices are developed to meet the requirements of the 'student experience'. The pursuit of knowledge is neither addressed nor mentioned.

Another development that demonstrates the rising prominence of 'student experience' in higher education is the creation and expansion of jobs that have the 'student experience' at their heart. Pro-Vice Chancellors of Student Experience, Student Support Officers, Student Experience Champions and Student Support Administrators have become part of the university, and the enhancing of the new 'student experience' is what keeps managers and many administrators occupied.

This managerial focus on 'student experience' means that the relationship between students and the institution will have to be regularly renegotiated and adapted. It is a development that illustrates the self-perpetuating nature of the 'student experience'.

The more universities are preoccupied with providing professional services to meet the 'student experience', the more the demands from students to improve or enhance that experience will increase and there will be less time to nurture the love of knowledge and understanding that is the purpose of a university. The integration of the 'student experience' into managerial structures sends the message that knowledge is no longer important.

On a national level, new developments such as the establishment of an Office for Students and the proposed Teaching Excellence Framework will consolidate the 'student experience' as the main focus of the university. The Office for Students will be responsible for overseeing funding, quality and standards as outlined in the *Higher Education and Research Bill 2016–17* (House of Commons Business, Innovation and Skills Committee 2016a) while the Teaching Excellence Framework will be introduced with the aims of assessing the quality of teaching and the student experience of teaching in all universities (House of Commons Business, Innovation and Skills Committee 2016b). Once new assessments are introduced universities will undoubtedly be ranked in order of performance and this will give the desire to be excellent in offering the 'student experience' even more momentum. The value of these and other assessments that have the 'student experience' at its heart are rarely questioned. But they should be. The National Student Satisfaction survey (NSS) which, in 2016, ranked leading institutions such as University of the Arts, London, and the London School of Economics and Political Science (LSE) towards the bottom (THE 2016) shows that these student-experience-based assessments have become ridiculous expressions of student whims, subjective judgements and feelings.

The fact that the value of these results and the subsequent rankings of such assessments are rarely questioned reveals the higher education sector's complacency and complicity in advocating the 'student experience'.

The introduction of the Teaching Excellence Framework displays the lack of trust by government in the ability of universities to provide a university education as autonomous institutions. If universities were trusted there would not be any need to introduce checks and controls on academics and higher education institutions.

The lack of trust displayed towards universities is symptomatic of a wider loss of direction that can be observed within the higher education sector. That there can be an emphasis on the 'student experience' reflects the decline of the authority of lecturers which, traditionally, was based on their subject knowledge. With the demise of knowledge-based education the traditional source of authority of lecturers has diminished.

In fact, student-centred education, by its very nature, diminished the authority of lecturers by asking them to listen to student opinions and to make all content relevant to their experiences. However, the idea of 'relevant knowledge' is deeply flawed because rather than introducing students to new and challenging ideas it reduces the content of teaching to what is perceived, often rather vaguely, as relevant to them. This traps students in the world they inhabit rather than providing them with an opportunity to develop their potential to the full by gaining knowledge and understanding of the world. When subjects, subject knowledge and the authority of lecturers are contested it means that universities have lost sight of the importance of the pursuit of knowledge and, therefore, of the purpose of a university.

How the 'student experience' was sold

Why have universities abandoned knowledge-based education in favour of student-centred education and learning-process-oriented teaching? The political or ideological shift in academic thinking that drives this development is the idea that knowledge-based education is elitist and privileges students that enter university with traditional academic qualifications (Young 2013). The students that are thought to lose out in a knowledge-based system are those who may hold different academic qualifications – such as BTECs – or are said to come from disadvantaged backgrounds. It is these 'non-traditional' students who are said to benefit from student-centred education as it focuses on processes of learning and the development of skills that it is believed this group needs.

Although the student-centred approach to education now extends to all students and has become the norm within higher education, the belief that removing elitist knowledge-based education helps non-traditional students succeed implies that there are differences in learning between traditional and non-traditional students and that they require special approaches to education, teaching and learning to succeed. In reality it stigmatizes these students and underrates their capacity to learn and think like any other student (Mieschbuehler 2017).

A 'manifesto' for moving beyond 'student experience'

In the short period of time when the 'student experience' has come to dominate university policies and practices and university education, a range of measures and initiatives has been introduced that, if they were to be abolished tomorrow, would mark the beginning of a shift beyond 'student experience' driven university education.

1) Abolish the National Student Survey

If universities want to return to knowledge-based education, a start could be made by abolishing the National Student Survey. The National Student Survey, introduced in 2005 by the Higher Education Funding Council in England (HEFCE), has become the annual event that celebrates the reorganisation of the university around students' subjective opinions and away from knowledge. The survey is circulated among final-year undergraduate students at all publicly funded higher-education institutions, and it is proclaimed to be 'a widely recognized authoritative survey' that 'gives students a powerful collective voice to help shape the future of their course and their university or college' (Ipsos MORI and HEFCE 2016).

What the National Student Survey actually does is make the experience, opinions and feelings of students more important than the authority and judgement of academics. It gives university management their own research-base that enables them to discipline lecturers and micromanage what is taught down to module level by demanding that teaching is restructured to enhance student satisfaction. The abolition of the National Student Survey would immediately rectify the annual distortion of academic life and open up the possibility of restoring the authority of academics. It would mean universities would have to begin focusing, not on what students feel they want, but what students need to develop intellectually. Most importantly it would mean that academics could teach their subject freely.

Abolishing the National Student Survey would shake up academia and would send a clear message to students that going to university should not make you satisfied like a trip to McDonald's but should make you intellectually dissatisfied so that you demand more knowledge and greater understanding. Experiences are not knowledge and the pursuit of knowledge is what universities are for.

2) No more 'student experience' posts

If student satisfaction was no longer assessed, it would automatically save lecturers time and effort. It would also minimize the inclination to increase the number of posts that already exist or are being invented to help enhance the 'student experience'.

But that is not enough. It is time to do away with all 'student experience' posts. No more Pro-Vice Chancellors of Student Experience, Student Support Officers, Student Experience Champions and Student Support Administrators.

Having fewer employees who are concerned with the 'student experience' would also reduce the current levels of policing staff are exposed to. Better still, the very suggestion that these posts should be abolished will open up a space for a renewed debate on what university is for. The National Student Survey cannot be abolished and 'student experience'-related employment cannot end unless academics and students are prepared to be provocative and start that debate.

3) No to the 'Office for Students' and the 'Teaching Excellence Framework'

The name says it all: the 'Office *for Students*'. Not the 'Office *for Universities*' or the 'Office *for Higher Education*'; the university is now all about the students and the 'student experience'. The national checks, controls and punitive sanctions that may come from the proposed Office for Students, and through the implementation of the Teaching Excellence Framework, will force university managers to drive the 'student experience' agenda forward in ways that will leave the knowledge-based university a fading memory. At the time of writing neither the Office for Students or the Teaching Excellence Framework are in place but they will be by 2017, 20 years on from the Dearing Report and the 'student experience' era that report helped create. They are not needed and they should be abolished.[1]

4) Bring back knowledge-based education

Probably the most objectionable consequence of the expansion of the 'student experience' is the decline in knowledge-based education in universities. Arguing for the reintroduction of liberal or knowledge-based education can seem like bringing back something from the past that may not be relevant for today's world. But knowledge-based education is and can be as modern as any other approach to education, including the student-centred approach, which is often misleadingly referred to as a progressive approach to education (see Kennedy, Chapter 4 in this volume).

Knowledge-based education is concerned with the acquisition of knowledge for its own sake and the development of the mind that results from knowledge (Hirst 1965). As Matthew Arnold famously wrote, the aim of this teaching is to learn 'the best that is known and thought in the world' (Arnold [1864] 2003: 50). In knowledge-based education all teaching must be rational and whatever is taught must be based on reason and logically consistent intelligent justifications (Newman [1873] 1960; Hirst 1965; Oakeshott 1989; Halstead 2005). Thoughts, ideas and theories must be presented in a way that leaves them open to critical and rational evaluation. The disinterested pursuit of knowledge, through the critical examination of alternative beliefs, is part of knowledge-based education and requires open-mindedness, impartiality and the willingness to revise opinions as new evidence emerges (Halstead 2005).

Knowledge-based education has been criticized for being elitist and over-emphasizing the academic study of subjects over other purposes of education (Martin 1994 cited in Mulcahy 2010; O'Hear 1981). This criticism has led to the introduction at all levels of education of 'normative commitments about what people ought to be like' (Mulcahy 2010: 7). These instrumental 'other purposes' of education, such as ensuring graduates are 'employable', 'environmentally aware' and committed to 'inclusion' and 'diversity', are now so commonplace that they seem to be part of the mission of the university. Newman in *The Idea of a University* argues, however, that 'knowledge is, not merely a means to something beyond it', it is 'an end sufficient to rest in and to pursue for its own sake', 'knowledge is capable of being its own end' (Newman [1873] 1960: 78).

It is time to bring knowledge back in to the university.

In the 'student experience' all is relative

But to teach knowledge we have to believe in it. In the university, relativism is rife. Hardly anyone believes in knowledge, and statements such as 'all truth is relative' pass without comment or criticism. The ubiquitous nature of relativism today is a result of a new phenomenon, 'cultural relativism', the widely accepted belief that all 'cultures' must be respected along with their unique value systems, which are accepted and acknowledged without comment or criticism. Relativism and cultural relativism together constitute an attack on knowledge (Hayes and Mieschbuehler 2015). Yet the university is the embodiment of Enlightenment values and has the unique educational function of advancing knowledge as well as teaching existing knowledge, although schools and colleges may also have that latter commitment. The way in which human knowledge and understanding is passed between generations, or advanced, is through knowledge-based education. If universities no longer believe in 'knowledge', they cannot pass it on and will have to resort to alternative educational aims, which partly explains the rise of the 'student experience' and student-centred education in universities, because for many relativists there is nothing but a myriad of incommensurate 'experiences'.

Relativism survives because of an academic culture that is favourable to it. The emphasis on 'experience' is the reason why relativism thrives. Talking about and interpreting experiences is a feature of student-centred education, and 'experience' dominates present national and institutional educational research. To undermine relativism, its self-contradictions can be pointed out. Probably the best-known self-contraction which can be used as a refutation of relativism has been provided by

Nozick (2001). He even refers to the example as a 'quick refutation' of relativism. Nozick showed that if someone argues that 'All truth is relative', this assertion is easily dismissed by asking, 'Is that view relative?' (Nozick 2001: 15). It shows that statements asserting the relativity of truth are self-refuting because relativists face a general problem. When relativists utter any statement, they must engage in 'truth talk'. For example, when relativists assert propositions like 'there is no universal truth to which our construction is a more or less good approximation', they engage in 'truth talk' (Bridges 1999: 610). Beyond simple self-contradictory statements, relativists also engage in 'truth talk' through their work; for example, when they state beliefs or discuss evidence. This propositional 'truth talk' also self-refutes the claim that all 'truth' is relative. These 'quick refutations' cannot be convincingly employed unless, through continual debate and discussion, an attempt is made to win the case for knowledge.

The argument for knowledge is based on the belief that we are rational human beings and as such 'it is incumbent on us to understand the reason for things, including the reasons for our conduct' (O'Hear 2009: 241). This belief requires teachers to initiate students into the inheritance of human achievement (Oakeshott 1989). Thoughts, ideas and theories must be presented in a way that leaves them open to critical and rational evaluation. The potential to inspire intellectual curiosity in students and a desire for their human heritage is the opposite of initiating them into the 'student experience'.

Beyond edutainment

The rise of the 'student experience' and the changes in university policies and practices, and in academic education, that have been introduced over the last two decades to meet the 'student experience' requirements have had a profound impact on the direction university education has taken. Universities are now preoccupied with concerns about student satisfaction and the student journey through university and into employment. To facilitate this they employ an army of people in student support services. Arum and Roksa described this new trend in education particularly with reference to teaching and learning as the preoccupation with 'the art of capturing audiences and entertaining them' (2011: 5). It is hard to disagree with them and to conclude that the 'student experience' is just *edutainment* and that would be something that students would reject if they saw it for what it was.

Students do not, or did not, think about their educational institutions in terms of providing the 'student experience'. Students go to university because they are passionate about a subject. Going to university may be packaged for them in terms of getting a job and being financially well off at some later date, but these instrumental motivations do not diminish the desire to get an education and to be intellectually challenged (Mieschbuehler 2017). This may soon change and students may eventually absorb the idea that university education is about them and their 'student experience'.

Likewise, academics do not think about their educational institutions as providing the 'student experience'. Academics are still passionate about their subjects. Many believe that, as Oakeshott (1989) says, when lecturers engage in their daily scholarly activities students learn from them without having to be explicitly taught. Academics are told by managers that 'employability' and graduate destinations are the new business of the university and they learn to be 'student-centred' on teacher training courses. They may, in time, also absorb the idea that university education is all about the 'student experience'. Let's hope not and that they maintain the belief that the real 'student experience' is the 'academic experience'.

Note

1 A positive sign that the Teaching Excellence Framework is not supported by students comes from a letter to *The Guardian* signed by many student unions and individual members of the National Union of Students: TEF is an unreliable test for university teaching, Letters, *The Guardian*, 10 August 2016: https://www.theguardian.com/educa tion/2016/aug/09/tef-is-an-unreliable-test-for-university-teaching (accessed 10/08/2016).

References

Arnold, M. ([1864] 2003) The function of criticism at the present time, in Collini, S. (ed.) *Culture and Anarchy and Other Writings*, Cambridge: Cambridge University Press: 26–57.

Arum, R. and Roksa, J. (2011) *Academically Adrift: Limited Learning on College Campuses*, Chicago and London: The University of Chicago Press.

Boghossian, P. (2007) *Fear of Knowledge: Against Relativism and Constructivism*, Oxford: Oxford University Press.

Bridges, D. (1999) Educational research: pursuit of truth or flight into fancy? *British Educational Research Journal*, 25(5): 597–616.

Dearing, R. (1997) *Report of the National Committee of Inquiry into Higher Education*, London: Department for Education and Employment: http://www.leeds.ac.uk/educol/ncihe/ (accessed 20/07/2016).

Ecclestone, K. and Hayes, D. (2008) *The Dangerous Rise of Therapeutic Education*, Abingdon, Oxon, and New York: Routledge.

Fox, C. (2002) The massification of higher education, in Hayes, D. and Wynyard, R. (eds.) *The McDonaldization of Higher Education*, Westport: Bergin and Garvey.

Halstead, M. (2005) Liberal values and liberal education, in Carr, W. (ed.) *The Routledge Falmer Reader in Philosophy of Education*, London: Routledge.

Haselgrove, S. (ed.) (1994) *The Student Experience*, The Society for Research into Higher Education, Buckingham: Open University Press.

Hayes, D. and Mieschbuehler, R. (2015) The refuge of relativism, in O'Grady, A. and Cottle, V. (eds.) *Exploring Education at Post-Graduate Level*, London: Routledge.

Hirst, P. H. (1965) Liberal education and the nature of knowledge, in Archambault, R. D. (ed.) *Philosophical Analysis and Education*, London: Routledge and Kegan Paul.

House of Commons Business, Innovation and Skills Committee (2016a) *Higher Education and Research Bill 2016–17*, London: The Stationery Office Ltd: http://services.parliament.uk/ bills/2016-17/highereducationandresearch.html (accessed 10/07/2016).

House of Commons Business, Innovation and Skills Committee (2016b) *The Teaching Excellence Framework: Assessing Quality in Higher Education*, London: The Stationery Office Ltd: www.publications.parliament.uk/pa/cm201516/cmselect/cmbis/572/572.pdf (accessed 11/ 08/2016).

Ipsos MORI and Higher Education Funding Council (HEFCE) (2016) *The National Student Survey*, London and York: Ipsos MORI and Higher Education Funding Council: http://www.thestudentsurvey.com/about.php/ (accessed 11/08/2016).

Letters (2016) TEF is an unreliable test for university teaching, Letters, *The Guardian*, 10 August: https://www.theguardian.com/education/2016/aug/09/tef-is-an-unreliable-test-for-university-teaching (accessed 20/08/2016).

Mieschbuehler, R. (2017) *The Minoritisation of Higher Education Students*, London and New York: Routledge (forthcoming).

Mulcahy, D. (2010) Redefining without undermining liberal education, *Innovative Higher Education*, 35(3): 203–214.

Newman, J. H. ([1873] 1960) *The Idea of a University*, Indiana: The University of Notre Dame Press.

Nozick, R. (2001) *Invariances: The Structure of the Objective World*, London: Harvard University Press.

Oakeshott, M. (1989) *The Voice of Liberal Education*, ed. by Fuller, T., London: Yale University Press.

O'Hear, A. (1981) *Education, Society and Human Nature: An Introduction to the Philosophy of Education*, London: Routledge.

O'Hear (2009) Education, value and the sense of awe, in O'Hear, A. and Sidwell, M. (eds.) *The School of Freedom: a Liberal Education Reader from Plato to the Present Day*, Exeter and Charlottesville: Imprint Academic.

Temple, P., Callender, C., Grove, L. and Kersh, N. (2014) *Managing the Student Experience in a Shifting Higher Education Landscape*, York: The Higher Education Academy.

Times Higher Education (THE) (2016) National Student Survey 2016: overall satisfaction results, World University Rankings, *Times Higher Education*, 10 August: https://www.timeshighereducation.com/student/news/national-student-survey-2016-overall-satisfaction-results (accessed 10/08/2016).

Williams, J. (2016) *Academic Freedom in an Age of Conformity: Confronting the Fear of Knowledge*, London and New York: Palgrave Macmillan.

Woodall, T., Hiller, A. and Resnick, S. (2014) Making sense of higher education: students as consumers and the value of the university experience, *Studies in Higher Education*, 39(1): 48–67.

Young, M. (2013) Overcoming the crisis in curriculum theory: a knowledge-based approach, *Journal of Curriculum Studies*, 45(2): 101–118.

9

BEYOND THE THERAPEUTIC UNIVERSITY

Dennis Hayes

In Blackwell's bookshop in Broad Street, Oxford, tourists can buy a small book edited by David Palfreyman which celebrates what is its title: *The Oxford Tutorial*. The title has a subheading: *'Thanks, You Taught Me How to Think'* (Palfreyman 2008). Coming back to Oxford in a few decades, if the therapeutic turn in education continues, it might well read 'Thanks, you taught me how to feel'.

The idea that we were seeing the creation of the 'therapeutic university' (Hayes and Wynyard 2002, Hayes 2004, Ecclestone and Hayes 2008a) was a way of strongly pointing out the possible future consequences of several dangerous therapeutic tendencies in education. Ironically, Ron Barnett saw the 'therapeutic university' in more positive terms as a conceptual development, a possible new vision of a university offering individual and social therapy to deal with (ontological) uncertainties about life as well as (epistemological) uncertainties about knowledge. The 'therapeutic university', in Barnett's sense, was a 'feasible utopia' already happening but 'unlikely fully to transpire' because of the 'countervailing forces – of self-interested entrepreneurialism and competitiveness in the positioning of universities into the global economy' (Barnett 2011: 129). That the university is becoming a competitive global business will not save it from the negative therapeutic turn or weaken the possibility of it becoming a therapeutic 'utopia'. The reason is that the therapeutic turn is not contradictory to but *complementary* to what Barnett and many other commentators see as 'marketization'. The therapeutic turn does not involve giving student 'consumers' what they want but offering them what seems like ways of resolving their (ontological) angst. While students are still subject to the 'market', they feel that everything focuses on them, on their concerns and their feelings. The same is true of many academics, administrative staff and managers who adopt therapeutic ideas and techniques while having to meet ever more demanding financial and business targets (see Ecclestone and Hayes 2008a, Chapters 5 and 6). Barnett even believes that the university itself is in need of 'social therapy' about its uncertain place in the world and how it could be 'better informed about itself' (Barnett 2011: 128), but the university in therapy could still be even more globally competitive.

If you believe, as Barnett has argued for over 15 years, that the university has a responsibility to 'add to uncertainty in the world *and* help assuage that uncertainty' (Barnett 2011: 123) both within us and without – in the world – then the logical conclusion must be that you believe in the creation of some form of 'therapeutic university'. Barnett, the leading writer on higher education of the present time, has powerfully articulated a philosophy for the 'therapeutic university', but it is possible to reject its foundational premise that the university has a responsibility to 'add to uncertainty in the world *and* help assuage that uncertainty' and to argue, using his terminology, that the university has only an 'epistemological' responsibility and that 'ontological' states are not its business. Its business is knowledge.

The attack on knowledge

The therapeutic turn in education can be explained as the increasing emphasis on emotion over the intellect. It might seem that Oxford, or any university, might be immune from the therapeutic turn as the duty of academia is primarily an intellectual one, the pursuit of knowledge and understanding. The existence of this pursuit is the real 'countervailing force' in the university both to 'marketization' and to the therapeutic term.

When *The Dangerous Rise of Therapeutic Education* was published in 2008, Lee Jones, in his review of the book, found the general thesis of a therapeutic turn convincing from the primary school to the further education college, but of the chapter on the 'therapeutic university' he said: 'the evidence for the therapeutic turn in higher education seems very weak. The chapter on universities contains a stirring defence of education for its own sake but also rails against fairly unobjectionable ideas and … reads as polemical' (Jones 2008).

It was easy to take the references to such things as counselling services and stress workshops as unobjectionable, but there were already pointers to something more profound that was going on. One example was a leaflet titled 'A Guide for Students – Counselling and Supervisory Services' from one university suggesting that students who study various subjects might encounter issues that require counselling:

> We are also aware of the different sorts of demands which different programmes of study make upon students, such as in the field of Health Care. For some people, a caring role at work can mean that they are always seen in this role, even outside work and so it can become hard to attend to their own needs and feelings … Similarly, the pressures of life in schools dealing with the issues of young people can make considerable emotional and physical demands on students in teacher education.
>
> Students studying in the disciplines of Psychology, Sociology or the Expressive arts may find themselves re-examining areas of their lives which

have previously seemed unproblematic to them. On the other hand, students working in competitive sports have other types of emotional issues to confront and resolve. For other people it is not a particular event that is bothering them but more a general feeling of anxiety, stress or feeling low.

(Ecclestone and Hayes 2008a: 91)

This leaflet was an early and explicit example of an institution going beyond paternalistic worries about the transitional stress of leaving home and making a new life and new friends, beginning to study as a student and then having to cope with examinations. The idea that academic disciplines might contain content that was psychologically unsettling has since become a major concern, not one that arises from the formal and informal institutional counselling industry but from students themselves.

While some of the unobjectionable practices have transformed into parodies of themselves with the emergence of 'puppy rooms' and 'petting zoos' at several universities where students can relieve their exam and other stresses by stroking a variety of furry creatures, the therapeutic turn has developed into what can only be called an 'attack on knowledge itself'.

Within the last two years, two major, and related, developments have begun to fundamentally change the epistemological basis of the university. The first is the call for 'trigger warnings' to be given about academic course material that someone considers potentially disturbing. The second is the demand that a university be a 'safe space'. The speed of this change is remarkable.

The idea that there is now a need for 'trigger warnings' to be given before any topic is discussed or work of art or literature that might be found by someone – a victim or someone who might, or might believe that someone might, potentially feel victimized – to be upsetting, first came to prominence because of a piece by the journalist Jenny Jarvie in the *New Republic* in March 2014. Despite a debate before her piece and after, in just over two years calls for 'trigger warnings' are everywhere and often in the top universities. Jarvie began by criticizing 'student leaders at the University of California, Santa Barbara, who passed a resolution urging officials to institute mandatory trigger warnings on class syllabi. Professors who present "content that may trigger the onset of symptoms of Post-Traumatic Stress Disorder" would be required to issue advance alerts and allow students to skip those classes' (Jarvie 2014). Then came calls for trigger warnings on Ovid, Shakespeare, Caravaggio, classical mythology, and a growing list of modern novels, including Chinua Achebe's masterpiece *Things Fall Apart,* as it might 'trigger' those who have experienced racism, colonialism and persecution or who don't like to be reminded of the horrors of history. In May 2016 the University of Oxford suggested trigger warnings for undergraduates on law courses if the material might be distressing for future lawyers and barristers. In a few years what seemed an isolated example of a therapeutic approach to academic study has begun to be institutionalized. Very soon giving 'trigger warnings', whether or not they are called by that name, could become common practice in universities as it already is in many student union blogs and publications. The publicity they have already received will also encourage self-censorship by lecturers. Why deal with material that might 'trigger' when it is easier to deal with mild and inoffensive topics? The quiet rejection of difficult or controversial may not even be noticed until someone writes about the 'Disneyfication' of academic courses and how they are carefully selected and 'safe'.

The complementary idea that universities should be 'safe spaces' where ideas can be discussed without antagonism or threat and without any mental or emotional upset has also begun to be accepted as good practice very quickly. The extent to which this idea had spread in universities was revealed by the first 'Free Speech University Rankings' (FSUR) produced by the on-line magazine spiked in February 2015 and repeated annually (see spiked 2016). Within a year it had led to what Tom Slater called the 'tyranny of safety':

> Safe Spaces originated in the women's and gay-liberation movements of the 1970s. Though they were often places of *physical* safety – whether it be from abusive partners or violent bigots – those spaces were also zones in which non-judgemental 'consciousness-raising' was preferred over forthright debate. But, nevertheless, they were seen as a means to an end – a place in which ideas, resources and tactics for changing the world outside could be developed. Today, Safe Spaces are the end. Sealing yourself off from the world – creating 'a home' in which 'victimised' undergraduates can take shelter, just for a few years – is what these alleged progressives pour all of their energies into.
>
> *(Slater 2016)*

What Jarvie concluded about trigger warnings applies equally to safe spaces, they are

> presented as a gesture of empathy, but the irony is they lead only to more solipsism, an over-preoccupation with one's own feelings – much to the detriment of society as a whole. Structuring public life around the most fragile personal sensitivities will only restrict all of our horizons. Engaging with ideas involves risk, and slapping warnings on them only undermines the principle of intellectual exploration.
>
> *(Jarvie 2014)*

The demand that the university become a 'safe space' from upsetting ideas might be a step towards helping students deal with their personal (ontological) uncertainties, but the consequence will be the loss of the university itself. It might seem that Barnett's 'feasible utopia' was coming into being, but the sudden speed of change has a more obvious and less philosophical cause.

In the eight years since *The Dangerous Rise of Therapeutic Education* was published, the generation of children and young people subject to state-sponsored therapeutic initiatives and a myriad of therapeutic fads and fashions have matriculated. The millennial generation brought up with years of Social and Emotional Aspects of Learning (SEAL) classes, anti-bullying initiatives, self-esteem building activities, destressing workshops, resilience training, happiness classes, brilliance training – all teaching them to value themselves and express their feelings and always, always, to ensure they are 'safe', have arrived at university and realized that it is not school and they feel they can't cope.

It is not their fault. The therapeutic turn in education was led by government and policymakers, by teachers and teacher trainers who prepared the ground for the millennials to want to have something that was all about them, their safety and their feelings, not a traditional university education but something celebrated by most universities as the 'student experience' (see Mieschbuehler, Chapter 8 in this volume). But this welcoming, supportive, paternalistic 'student experience' organized by institutions rather than the students themselves turned out not to be enough. As we have seen, the most vocal millennials did not want anything in the 'academic experience', in the curriculum, that offended their fragile sensibilities.

It would be an exaggeration to say that all universities have taken the therapeutic turn, but what we can say is that the recent clamour for 'trigger warnings' and 'safe spaces' is just the beginning, and universities have been taken by surprise. Many academics believe that the pursuit of knowledge and understanding can continue as it has for centuries. They keep their heads down and try to go on working without challenging the new 'student-centred' teaching with its aim of a better 'student experience'. However, there are a few people – often working and writing outside of the university – who challenge the therapeutic turn, and they have deliberately given the millennials the 'offensive' label the 'Snowflake Generation' (see Fox 2016).

The Snowflake Generation goes to university

Now that the Snowflake Generation is at university, do universities and academics have to capitulate to their demands? In a therapeutic culture this may happen without any directly stated intension to adopt a therapeutic approach. Adaptations and activities in response to imagined possible claims or real claims of anxiety, vulnerability and offence arise spontaneously (Ecclestone and Hayes 2008a: 133). One aspect of the demands of the Snowflake Generation that weakens their force is the contradictory nature of the claim to be vulnerable along with the authoritarian nature of their demands. They 'demand' protection and campaign against anyone who they feel is offensive – seeking to get them disciplined, removed from posts or sacked. This has earned them another designation as 'cry-bullies'. As Matthew Parris has pointed out, the presentation of the self as a victim, someone who suffers, 'brooks no contradiction. It confers upon the sufferer a dignity, and a kind of authority, elevating him or her above reproach' (Parris 1996 cited in Ecclestone and Hayes 2008a: 10). Yet like Claire Fox, who in her polemic *I Find That Offensive!* (2016: ix–xxii), saw the welling up of tears and obvious upset among young people taking part in debates as something of a surprise, even a shock. They seem to take any criticism, especially that of their often conventional ideas, personally. What most people find unobjectionable, the snowflakes see as a terrible faux pas which can cause real distress to them. Fox gives the example of the emotional response she engendered by saying 'Mohammed' rather than '*The Prophet* Mohammed' in a discussion about free speech and Charlie Hebdo murders (Fox 2016: x). Try suggesting to students that dyslexia is a contested concept despite all their dyslexia certificates, or that they are not stuck in the 'learning styles' box of 'kinaesthetic learners', or that they are not determined in their potential or ambitions by their religious, cultural or class identities, and see the offence and upset you cause. It is not only against challenging argument that the emotional response seems appropriate but against any expression or question over-heard and labelled a 'microaggression'. Be careful if you ask of almost anyone 'Where are you from?' or 'Where did you go on holiday?' or 'Can I help with that?' because you might be revealing yourself as someone with 'unconscious' racist, classist/privileged or sexist views. The unintentional nature of offence in such questions empowers those who claim hurt and allows them to express moral outrage:

> The focus on the unconscious or unwitting dimension of micro-aggression is important. People accused of this misdemeanour are not indicted for what they have done nor for what they said, and not even for what they think they think, but for their unconscious thoughts. It does not matter what a micro-aggressor intended – what counts is that someone claims that they were insulted or traumatised by their gestures or words. The denunciation of micro-aggressions has meshed seamlessly with the obsessive search for harmful gestures and words associated with everyday sexism and racism. Micro-aggression offers a moral resource on which the performance of outrage can draw.
>
> *(Furedi 2016)*

In the infantilized world of the Snowflake Generation they demand that 'mummy and daddy' – someone in authority – must punish those who hurt their feelings. A natural response to their activities among young people who do not want to be infantilized is to become 'anti-snowflakes'.

Being anti-snowflake and giving the snowflakes a taste of their own medicine may seem like fun. Trolling the trolls, labelling the feminists 'feminazis' or calling for the banning, dismissal or sacking of the more authoritarian snowflakes because they call for the banning, dismissal or sacking of others. Claire Fox, who has for over a decade organized, hosted and chaired hundreds of sixth-form debates in the Institute of Ideas *Debating Matters* competition, makes this appeal based on that experience to all young people, including the snowflakes and anti-snowflakes:

> I end with a call to arms for you all, because I can't give up on the Snowflakes just yet: you're young, you have time to change. You all need to toughen up and make a virtue of the right to be offensive. It's an easy sentence, but actually it's a challenge: take hold of your destiny and sort out this mess. Whether you are Snowflakes or Anti-Snowflakers, you need to learn the trick of turning subjective outrage into measured, passionate, coherent argument capable of

convincing others, rather than retreating into your respective self-erected camps, whether safe-space bubbles or free speech echo chambers. You have a chance to shape the future as you want it, independent of and in defiance of the contemporary mood of fear and loathing.

(Fox 2016: 178)

Perhaps this is the best you can do as far as appeals to young people go. But a similar appeal needs to be made to all academics, administrative and managerial staff in universities.

Beyond vulnerability

The first step in challenging the therapeutic turn is simply to make academics and others aware of the therapeutic turn. Because the turn to therapy is spontaneous, in therapy culture it goes unnoticed. An example from my own experience will illustrate what I mean. I was speaking at an academic freedom debate and had prepared a press release which I sent to the press office at my university. It came back in a final draft for me to see with one single addition: 'Of course free speech and academic freedom have to be balanced with *the need to protect vulnerable young minds*' [emphasis added]. Needless to say that addition was removed but the press officer who wrote it did not do it with any intension of deliberately undermining what I had written about the importance of free speech and academic freedom. It just seemed the right thing to add. Similarly it just seems natural to assume students will be nervous and anxious about coming to university, that they will find course work and examinations stressful to a point at which they might even become mentally ill. But going to university, gaining knowledge and understanding and showing what you know should be the most exciting and welcome things in a young person's life? Academics and others need to stop thinking of students as vulnerable. They may be helped in this if they see that there exists an unarticulated or poorly articulated philosophy of human nature which this spontaneous assumption of vulnerability expresses. This is the philosophy of a diminished self which is incapable of moral and ascetic self-denial in order to realize human potential and achieve noble and great things (see Ecclestone and Hayes 2008a: 135–144). In its latest formulation by the UK government, this diminished concept of human being is expressed in the worry that we all might be mentally ill, using a definition of 'mentally ill' that pathologizes ordinary mood swings and concerns and even incidents of what they call 'conduct disorder' (O'Neill 2016). Students are not a subcategory of the 'mentally ill'.

The irony is that 'trigger warnings' and 'safe spaces' have the opposite of their intended effect. The same is true of anti-bullying, happiness and 'well-being' and similar initiatives. Trigger warnings, by seeking to avoid issues that are distressing, actually make the distress more permanent and, if it is serious, much worse (see Lukianoff and Haidt 2015). Constant sensitizing of young people to issues like 'stress' and 'bullying' will bring them to feel stressed and feel bullied about issues that previously were not seen as anything to bother about. Perhaps the concern with 'happiness' and 'happiness classes' is the most telling example. The more you seek to be happy the more miserable you are going to be. Happiness comes as a by-product of serious engagement with the external world and never from internal soul-searching (see Ecclestone and Hayes 2008a: 158–160). If students seek a 'safe space' they are not going to come out and face the real world. They are choosing it for life but for a diminished and pathetic life.

The more vocal and belligerent of those who cry that they are offended and hurt on behalf of themselves or other 'victims' may seem to be raging against an oppressive system when in reality they are mostly affluent middle-class students and their middle-class academic cheerleaders. The writer and journalist Patrick West judges them very harshly:

> Today we live not so much in an 'age of rage', but in an age of tantrums, fuelled by the spoilt, privileged and make-believe victims. This is why they use babyish language, such as 'being offended' or 'being hurt' by what other people say. They have Safe Spaces and trigger warnings. They speak the language of passive victimhood, not revolutionary activism.
>
> *(West 2016)*

West may be correct about the childish desire the belligerent victims have for validation of their victimhood, but labelling their outburst 'tantrums' actually ignores the very real damage they do to academic life.

The tantrums almost always relate to an attempt to undermine knowledge and argument. The therapeutic turn in education was a dual attack on the subject. It was an attack on the human subject which was diminished and replaced with victim status and an attack on the curriculum subject, on the various forms into which human knowledge was divided and taught. Attacking knowledge was also an attack on the human subject as a knowing subject and its replacement with an emotional subject (Ecclestone and Hayes 2008b).

The Snowflake Generation of students have internalized this attack on the subject and are actively encouraging both victimhood and the rejection of knowledge. Whether or not they are so-called 'Social Justice Warriors' (SJWs), they claim that some knowledge is too distressing to have, some books should not be taught and that only certain people with a certain victim identity can even argue about a topic. On campuses around the world a man cannot discuss abortion because he hasn't got a uterus, white men cannot discuss racism or heterosexuals discuss gay rights and so on (Stanley 2014, O'Neill 2015, Gillespie 2016, Lesh 2016). Only certain things can be known and read, only certain things can be said as far as SJWs are concerned. They have little influence and we could just ignore their tantrums, but university authorities capitulate to them, and many academics are silent SJWs. Most educationalists – writers on education, policy makers and teacher trainers – believe that education should be political and that its end is not to learn 'the best that is known and thought' (Arnold [1864] 2003: 50) but to promote social justice. On a daily basis this belief means that only certain ideas and topics are acceptable, those that are inoffensive and safe. Argument is replaced by learning the truths of social justice, and those that disagree with those 'truths' are not to be argued with but given awareness therapy. It creates quietude on campus without the need for any strident SJW hectoring.

The real damage done to the university by the therapeutic turn is the death of debate, and the Snowflake Generation is trying to put the final nails in the coffin. The dual attack on the human subject as a knowing subject requires the restriction of debate because it is only through debate that knowledge and understanding can develop. A caveat is necessary here about what is meant by 'debate'. In a conversation with an educational advisor recently about organizing a debate between two schools, he said 'You don't mean debate in the old-fashioned sense where one side argues for a proposition and one against?' I replied 'Yes exactly, I meant good old-fashioned *debate*!' 'Debate' for the educational advisor was a form of therapeutic self-expression in a form becoming prevalent everywhere. A panel of young people each speak with emotion about some topic and the 'adult' audience applauds. The more personal and emotional the speech is, the louder the applause. This patronizing activity shows a real contempt for young people's intellectual abilities however flattering they may find the applause.

Towards the Socratic university

How do we go beyond the 'therapeutic university', which is now very likely to transpire? A university was traditionally the place where the defining activity was the pursuit of knowledge and understanding without fear or favour. That pursuit required knowledge of the best that has been 'known and thought' (Arnold [1864] 2003: 50) in a discipline and the pursuit of new knowledge based on this required argument and experimentation. Academia is currently in a state of what Socrates in the *Phaedo* calls 'misology', an immoral situation where the value of knowledge has been lost because of distaste for argument. It is an appalling situation for individuals as '[n]o greater misfortune can happen to anyone than that of developing a dislike for argument' (*Phaedo* [s89d] in Plato 1993: 151) and worse for academia as the societal embodiment of the belief in the power of argument and debate to reach the truth.

The university has to be recreated as a place where argument happens all the time, endlessly and with no restrictions on debate. In the *Apology*, Socrates presents a possible picture of life after death as an eternity of argument with the greatest heroes and poets:

> [A]bove all I should like to spend my time there, as here, in examining and searching people's minds, to find out who is really wise among them, and who only thinks that he is. What would one not give, gentlemen, to be able to scrutinize the leader of that great host against Troy, or Odysseus, or Sisyphus, or the thousands of other men and women whom one could mention, their

company and conversation – like the chance to examine them – would be unimaginable happiness?

(*Apology [s41bc] Plato 1993: 66*)

This vision of death as the 'unimaginable happiness' of examining and searching people's minds for all eternity is a vision of the university. It is the moral duty of everyone in the university to ensure that argument and debate goes on non-stop. Knowledge is a value, an end in itself, and not something sought for other instrumental purposes. It is 'the best thing' a human being can do:

> I tell you that to let no day pass without discussing goodness and all the other subjects about which you hear me talking and examining both myself and others is really the very best thing that a man can do, and that a life without this sort of examination is not worth living, you will be even less inclined to believe me.

(*Apology [s38ab] Plato 1993: 66*)

Socrates is often quoted out of context as saying that 'the unexamined life is not worth living', which in the context of the therapeutic turn can easily be seen a call for introspection and navel-gazing. In its original context above it is a call for argument, a call to talk and examine your ideas and those of others every day.

If life in higher education is to be worth living, the therapeutic turn has to be recognized and rejected in favour of a Socratic turn. It is something every academic can do. They can argue and criticize everything, and there are encouraging signs that a Socratic turn is possible. In both the UK and USA, campus free speech campaigns are having some success (see Chapter 1), and 2016 began well when Professor Louise Richardson became the first woman to be Vice-Chancellor of the University of Oxford in January 2016. Speaking to the *Telegraph* in the week of her appointment she said:

> We need to expose our students to ideas that make them uncomfortable so that they can think about why [*sic*] it is that they feel uncomfortable about and what it is about those ideas that they object to. And then to have the practice of framing a response and using reason to counter these objectionable ideas and to try to change the other person's mind and to be open to having their own minds changed.
>
> That's quite the opposite of the tendency towards safe spaces and I hope that universities will continue to defend the imperative of allowing even objectionable ideas to be spoken.

(*Espinoza 2016*)

Richardson was speaking at a time when the government's *Prevent Duty* required (from 21 September 2015) all universities to monitor external speakers in order that vulnerable students could not be radicalized – part of a strategy that cleverly uses the therapeutic turn to intervene in university life (see Hayes 2012). She was equally uncompromising on this:

> I think universities, if you like, are the best places in which to hear objectionable speech because you can counter it. If you allow reasonable counter arguments to those views you will delegitimise [them] and that's what a university should do.

The Socratic university has an academic champion of some distinction and influence in Richardson. Academics should not live in fear of the hemlock but be like her.

References

Arnold, M. ([1864] 2003) The function of criticism at the present time, in Collini, S. (ed.) *Culture and Anarchy and Other Writings*, Cambridge: Cambridge University Press: 26–57.

Barnett, R. (2011) The therapeutic university, in *Being a University*, Abingdon, Oxon, and New York, NY: Routledge: 120–130.

Ecclestone, K. and Hayes, D. (2008a) *The Dangerous Rise of Therapeutic Education*, Abingdon, Oxon, and New York, NY: Routledge.

Ecclestone, K. and Hayes, D. (2008b) Affect: knowledge, communication, creativity and emotion, *Beyond Current Horizons*: http://www.beyondcurrenthorizons.org.uk/affect-knowledge-communication-creativity-and-emotion/ (accessed 19 August 2016).

Espinoza, J. (2016) Extremist groups must be allowed to preach on British campuses, new Oxford head says, *Telegraph*, 16 January: http://www.telegraph.co.uk/education/educationnews/12102509/Extremist-groups-must-be-allowed-to-preach-on-British-campuses-new-Oxford-head-says.html (accessed 19 August 2016).

Fox, C. (2016) *'I Find That Offensive!'*, London: Biteback Publishing.

Furedi, F. (2016) The end of argument, *Prospect*, 21 January: http://www.prospectmagazine.co.uk/features/the-end-of-argument-university-speakers-protests-censorship-free-speech (accessed 19 August 2016).

Gillespie, T. (2016) The racialism of Rhodes must fall, spiked, 22 February: http://www.spiked-online.com/newsite/article/the-racialism-of-rhodes-must-fall/18058#.V7iIKJgrLIU (accessed 19 August 2016).

Hayes, D. (2004) The therapeutic turn in education, in Hayes, D. (ed.) *The Routledge Guide to Key Debates in Education*, London and New York, NY: Routledge: 180–185.

Hayes, D. (2012) Stop policing the university, spiked, 1 November: http://www.spiked-online.com/newsite/article/13044#.V7q_zZgrLIU (accessed 19 August 2016).

Hayes, D. and Wynyard, R. (eds.) (2002) *The McDonaldization of Higher Education*, Westport, CT: Bergin and Garvey.

Jarvie, J. (2014) Trigger happy, *New Republic*, 4 March: https://newrepublic.com/article/116842/trigger-warnings-have-spread-blogs-college-classes-thats-bad (accessed 19 August 2016).

Jones, L. (2008) Therapy culture and its critics, Culture Wars, 2 October: http://www.culturewars.org.uk/index.php/site/article/critical_therapy_culture/ (accessed 19 August 2016).

Lesh, M. (2016) Identity politics is the enemy of equality, spiked, 3 May: http://www.spiked-online.com/newsite/article/identity-politics-is-the-enemy-of-equality/18313#.V7iHYJgrLIU (accessed 19 August 2016).

Lukianoff, G. and Haidt, J. (2015) The codling of the American mind, *The Atlantic*, September: http://www.theatlantic.com/magazine/archive/2015/09/the-coddling-of-the-american-mind/399356/ (accessed 19 August 2016).

O'Neill, B. (2015) Never mind Rhodes – it's the cult of the victim that must fall, spiked, 28 December: http://www.spiked-online.com/newsite/article/never-mind-rhodes-its-the-cult-of-the-victim-that-must-fall/17762#.V7iIvJgrLIU (accessed 19 August 2016).

O'Neill, B. (2016) We're all mental patients now, spiked, 18 February: http://www.spiked-online.com/newsite/article/were-all-mental-patients-now/18045#.V7q_dZgrLIU (accessed 19 August 2016).

Palfreyman, D. (2008) *The Oxford Tutorial: 'Thanks, You Taught Me How to Think'* (Second Edition), Oxford: Oxford Centre for Higher Education Policy Studies: http://oxcheps.new.ox.ac.uk/Publications/Resources/OxCHEPS_OP1_08.pdf (accessed 19 August 2016).

Plato (1993) *The Last Days of Socrates*, Translated by Tredennick, H. and Tarrant, H., Harmondsworth: Penguin.

Slater, T. (2016) The tyranny of safe spaces, spiked, 15 January: http://www.spiked-online.com/newsite/article/the-tyranny-of-safe-spaces/17933#.V3EIG7grLIU (accessed 19 August 2016).

spiked (2016) Free speech university rankings, spiked: http://www.spiked-online.com/free-speech-university-rankings/results (accessed 19 August 2016).

Stanley, T. (2014) Oxford students shut down abortion debate. Free speech is under assault on campus, *Telegraph*, 19 November: http://www.telegraph.co.uk/news/politics/11239437/Oxford-students-shut-down-abortion-debate.-Free-speech-is-under-assault-on-campus.html (accessed 19 August 2016).

West, P. (2016) The age of belligerent victimhood, spiked, 19 August: http://www.spiked-online.com/newsite/article/the-age-of-belligerent-victimhood/18665#.V7hg4ZgrLIV (accessed 19 August 2016).

10

BEYOND PRAGMATISM

The pedagogy of the impressed

Austin Williams

Everybody loves China these days, but it has not always been thus. Its transformation from an international pariah state to the envy of the world has been even quicker and more impressive than its much-vaunted economic miracle. Emerging from a peasant economy to be the largest trading nation in the world in 35 years is astonishing, but its shift from Tiananmen Square revilement to gaining a seat on the UN Human Rights council in 25 years is no less remarkable. The strategic analyst Gerald Segal published an article in *Foreign Affairs* in 1999 titled 'Does China Matter?' As *The Diplomat* magazine now points out, 'today virtually nobody would ask the question'.

China and Chinese-ness are everywhere. The phrase 'Chinese Dream' has almost entered the Western canon. China's movie industry is gaining fans as well as providing a source of funding for ailing Western studios. Jack Ma's Alibaba is the most popular destination for online shopping worldwide. And the UN World Tourism Organization predicts that China will be the world's leading travel destination around 2016–2018.

Admittedly, there are still Cold Warriors who baulk at the continued use of Mao's face on China's paper currency, or who protest at the illiberal excesses of its one-party state, but it seems that, in general, we're all Chinaphiles now. Former British Prime Minister David Cameron is explicit: 'We want to see China succeed' (Cameron 2012).

Nowhere is China emerging as a Western obsession more than in the education sector. China's educational development – or its 'education revolution' as it is often approvingly dubbed – is cited as the way forward for many educationalists and politicians alike. As the West chases the Chinese yuan and tries to safeguard the financial benefits of luring Chinese students to its universities, it might be an appropriate time to explore the reality of Chinese education and what drives it. Maybe then we can understand the West's infatuation.

Undoubtedly, China's education sector has a scale, a speed of growth and a rigour that are breathtaking, and it is easy to be carried away by the numbers:

- Presently, there are 400 million school students in the state system.
- 31 million of those are currently engaged in higher education.[1]
- Every year, 9 million Chinese students take the national university entrance exam.
- This year, 7.25 million students will graduate – more than seven times that in 2000.
- Approximately 50,000 European students are making exchange agreements: around 7,600 from France, 5,500 from Germany and 24,000 from America.
- About 3,000 UK students attend Chinese universities in full or partial exchange programmes.

While there are many positive aspects of China's educational advances – the rise of literacy (the United Nations states that China is on track to provide 'near universal youth literacy' by 2015), the students' legendary work ethic, their clear desire for knowledge, or the intrepid nature of 350,000 young adults leaving home and taking up graduate positions across the world every year, for example – it might be worth providing some perspective on the less flattering side of Chinese education culture to see what the West is uncritically buying into. For example, the numbers are huge because China's population is so vast; in fact, a review of the global educational scene points out 'in comparison with other developed countries, (China's) enrolment rate is low' (Altbach *et al.* 2013: 126). And as one wag recently asked, "If it is all so good, why are so many trying to get into foreign universities?"

Whatever the criticism, China's educational ambitions are impressive. It has been less than 30 years since China passed a law requiring nine years of compulsory education, and this was only finally achieved in the late 1990s. Therefore, to castigate Chinese education might seem churlish given its dramatic successes, but this article aims to reveal some truths and also to focus criticism on the blind onward rush of Western educators to seize on a data analysis of Chinese performance standards as evidence that we can – and should – learn from their success.

The creativity gap

The classic image of the hard-working, early-achieving Chinese child prodigy actually reveals that creativity is usually allied to junior school status, i.e., child prodigies tend to be children, after all. Once in secondary school, Chinese kids are expected to stop such frivolity and give themselves over to a dedicated study of the curriculum. Many commentators are rightly concerned that too many students in the West extend their junior school 'playfulness' throughout their secondary and tertiary education and as a result do not have the basic foundations for serious study that comes from rote knowledge of certain key data. At least, they say, China provides the building blocks of understanding that seem to have been forgotten in the West.

True. But in China, it goes too far the other way: once students enter high school, personal creativity and individual expressiveness are marginalized. Once a student reaches the age of ten or so, having done the requisite music grades or imaginative artistic exploration, the violin and the paintbrush are put aside. For the next six or seven years, most don't play instruments, draw, read novels or do sport from that day onwards.

When applying for university places for arts subjects, for example, it is not uncommon for 19-year-old Chinese university interviewees to present portfolios containing crayon drawings or photos of glove puppets made when they were eight or nine. An incredulous Western question 'Why?' will be met with the self-conviction that they haven't had any time in the previous ten years to do a drawing for pleasure, relying instead on something that they created before serious schooling started. For a large majority of school students, such 'creative' activities are distractions from homework. While we should be rightly critical of the diminishment of Western educational standards and the over-infatuation with self-indulgent 'reflective learning', let us not over-flatter the technical rigidity of China.

Admittedly, many students do take to the arts, write, draw and play the piano, but as in the West, there is a class-based difference between middle-class city residents' and rural workers' educational priorities. As a recent academic paper points out: 'The struggle to succeed in urban China's educational arms race … or to master musical instruments or classical art forms, was seen as befitting only people of the requisite kind of quality – that is, those with urban status' (Griffiths and Jesper 2014). Rural dwellers are obviously more likely to prioritize what China deems to be the essentials and see creativity as an ill-afforded luxury. One teacher, when asked why Chinese children find it hard to provide estimates – rough answers to mathematical problems – said, 'I do not know why we have to teach estimation. Asking children to guess will not help them to get the correct answer. Then, they will not calculate seriously. I am also afraid that parents will query my teaching too' (Ng 2014: 21).

Where creativity is taught, it is frequently as a mechanical skillset, even in arts subjects. For instance, most Chinese school students learn an impressive set of technical artistic skills, but counterintuitively, many of them still only have a limited ability to draw. In fact, Chinese students are taught to draw particular objects in a 'correct' way. Their still life studies, for example, express a delightful capability in pencil shading; Impressionist landscapes are carried out in water colours and each one displays a beautiful mastery of technique that is hard to fault. This homogenization of artistic excellence is achieved by teaching each student to draw the same object for days and weeks until they 'get it right'. Students can often draw *this* bottle or *that* landscape correctly, but if they are asked to draw a different object, a different scene, very often they can't or won't do it. Chinese arts education simply gets students to hone visual memorization and formalistic technique. This is a neat trick and an impressive skill but not the same thing as free interpretation, which is what sketching, or art, should be about (Williams 2013b).

This is not to imply that Chinese are unable to be creative. Some students excel in creative professions, although many of the better students are returnees from sojourns to Western universities, so-called sea-turtles, those that have absorbed a little of the Western liberal traditions and have returned to their own shores. Even so it shows that poor creativity is not innate. Instead, it is clear that their contemporary social *environs* are largely responsible for narrowing their educational development, mainly because it refuses to allow 'autonomous thinking'. This is not the same thing as the over-indulged Western notion of 'creative thinking' or 'creative intelligence' (which in the West is often a euphemism for what Heidegger called 'subjective arbitrariness', intuitive thinking that dismisses the need for such trivial things as tuition and comprehension). Sometimes Western creative thinking has little to do with thinking ... or even the difficult business of creativity.

But in China, it is an equal and opposite problem. In China, while education is geared to understanding the world in order to learn from it, there is only limited access to that world. More importantly, the notion that you can freely interpret or critically comprehend the world is absent. In Leslie Chang's popular novel *Factory Girls*, she explores the Assembly Line attitude to learning, admittedly geared to poor migrants:

> After learning the alphabet and the phonetic sounds of the language, a student sat at a machine while columns of English words rotated past. The student read aloud each word and wrote it down without knowing what it meant, week after week, until he attained the highest speed. He then proceeded to another machine that showed Chinese definitions of words; next he advanced to short sentences. When a student achieved the top speed – able to write six hundred English sentences in one hour – he graduated to basic grammar. Only then did he learn the meaning of the words, phrases and sentences he had been repeating for months.
>
> *(Chang 2009: 282)*

The conditions of autonomy required for genuine critical thinking in China do not yet exist (notwithstanding the fact that terms like 'self-criticism' have resonances of the Cultural Revolution when ritualized state humiliation of teachers and professors was common: teachers, bound and gagged by their students, were forced to recant (to self-criticize) their errant pro-capitalist ways before being encouraged to jump from balconies). In the Western postmodern model, teachers are less physically threatened but still nervous about what and how to teach in syllabi that 'reject hierarchies ... and [see] all forms of 'reality' as arbitrary constructs' (Buchanan 2012).

In this Western model, critical enquiry regularly refers to what Professor Graham Good describes as the 'divisive categorisation' of identity politics that simply corrodes universal meaning. It is 'a profound skepticism towards human potential to comprehend the world' (Hammond 2007: 5). China's is a society that holds little store in self-awareness, and in order to develop an understanding of what it means, they are looking westwards to borrow a safe sense of selfhood from countries where identity infatuation is mainstream. The Western model of individualism in education has led to an increasingly relativized conceptualization of knowledge, and so China is sucking up lots of bad habits as well as good from its pedagogical plundering of Western universities.

In both universes, meaningful judgment is missing. In China, due to the pervasive nature of societal management, judgment is deemed to be impossible. In the West, due to the increased existence of relativized educational values, it is often deemed to be irrelevant.

As a result, the ability to critically engage, to take initiative, to apply knowledge, to challenge and to critique is somewhat alien to contemporary Chinese education, although things are changing somewhat. The new Code of Conduct for Chinese primary and middle school students encourages students to '[t]hink and question, be inquisitive. Pay attention in class and be forthright in expressing your opinion' (Han 2014). However, a society which, over the last 100 years, has frowned upon meaningful criticism will necessarily produce students who continue to skirt this injunction. One article describes a school visit in Shenzhen: 'From the first day of school, students who ask questions are silenced and those who try to exert any individuality are punished' (Xueqin 2011). Another research study found that 'asking questions and beginning discussions during class without first being authorized by the teacher would not always be rewarded. It might, on the contrary, be understood as being disrespectful to the teacher ... a violation of a moral principle or standard that is supposed to secure order and harmony in society' (Kirkebæk, Du and Jensen 2013: 8)

Unsurprisingly, as China develops and becomes more aware of the world, more and more Chinese parents feel that the school system is letting their children down. But this doesn't mean that they are progressively turning against relentless tuition and rote learning. Typically those who turn to home schooling do so to provide a more comfortable environment for dedicated, all-encompassing, carbon-copy regurgitation of the official school syllabus. It is a choice for those who simply feel that their children are not being spoon-fed with sufficient attention to detail in an overcrowded school system. Increasing numbers of parents are sending their kids to international schools, primarily to get a head start into the global marketplace with a Western education. We in the West may cringe, even more so because they aim for a 'creative' education for purely pragmatic reasons. Getting into a foreign university is essential so that students can insert the treasured Western tickbox on their CV. How they get there is irrelevant, and many charlatan 'international schools' are taking advantage.

It is reasonably well documented that poor students will use money, agents, parents, hooks or crooks to get into a recognizably named university regardless of their ability to cope when they get there. It is also reasonably well-documented that more Western universities are prepared to accept them!

The Global Times recently reported that many Chinese-run international schools teach a faux foreign curriculum. Zhang Fan, a manager at Beijing New Oriental

School, explained that 'although they were often successful in helping students to attain the grades they required to be admitted to an overseas university, they often did not provide a well-rounded education, meaning that their students would be woefully unprepared for studying abroad' (quoted in Xinyuan 2014).

In one interview with student Xu Peng, an engineering graduate from a lowly provincial town who made it to Tsinghua University in Beijing, he explained that the unstructured nature of university life took some adjusting to. 'There are no rules here … I was so confused during first semester, because nobody told me what to do' (Larmer 2014). Similarly, an architecture student likened the news that she had passed the Gaokao to being released from a prison sentence, only to find that – like many institutionalized prisoners – she 'couldn't handle freedom'. She instinctively pulled back from taking intellectual and conceptual risks for fear of standing out in a crowd or doing the wrong thing. It was much easier, she said, to do what everyone else was doing, using them as benchmarks of acceptable pass-grade behaviour.

Technical technique

Sinophile marketing guru Tom Doctoroff says 'the only way to get ahead   and everybody needs to get ahead in China – is to master the rules' (quoted in Joshi 2010). Indeed, China's technocratic impulse, derived from centuries of social advancement ordained by the Confucian examination system, is still predominantly a mechanistic device to get a job. This sits very easily with the Western paradigm that simply argues for education as an instrumental opportunity to develop employability skills.

In this regard, there is a certain circularity in this debate: China is looking at a West that is desperately looking to China. Both are unaware that each is looking at a wish-fulfilment reflection of itself. The result will be an intellectual stalemate that will undoubtedly result in technocratic apology for real education.

In a recent survey of 250 Beijing students, almost '90 percent of applicants said they had submitted fraudulent recommendation letters, and half had used false transcripts' (Marcus 2013). The Programme for International Student Assessment (PISA) results – that have become the most envied evidence of China's rise – are OECD-sponsored tables that compare the performance of 15-year-olds across the world in standardized tests in mathematics, science and reading. Students from Shanghai have the top scores of every category; as a result, ex-Under Secretary of State for Education, Elizabeth Truss MP, said that the UK will implement maths hubs in England (not the entire UK) along the lines of Shanghai lesson plans in order to raise its own standards (the UK is currently languishing in 26th place in maths, although in 2003 it was disqualified due to a low response rate).

PISA tests are comparative assessments of countries across the world. Much has been written of the anomaly of having the city of Shanghai used as 'representative' of China in the PISA tests – ironically, precisely because of the patchy performance of education in some of China's rural backwaters. Secondly, to be 'cultured' in the

West (Thomas Mann's 'cultivated man') is to imply a knowledge of the arts, to speak another language, etc. To be cultured in China is to know mathematics. One academic study from Hong Kong shows that beyond school, 'Chinese parents hold high expectations of academic achievement and tend to play an active role in helping children to learn mathematics' (Ng 2010: 26). For Truss to laud this Shanghainese 'anomaly' suggests that she has gone native as PISA tests do nothing to illuminate the meaning of education. Frank Furedi has noted that 'PISA is interested in literacy but not in understanding the meaning of literature' (Furedi 2013). So while Shanghai students are at the top of PISA reading tests, for many in China 'reading' is a technical skill with no direct correlation to comprehension – and to read for pleasure is often deemed to be an impractical indulgence.

As such, PISA results are a (useful) dataset recording a comparison of specific test results. But comparing Cheshire with China needs a bit of nuance. If you compare Korea with China – which at least has a similar hierarchical system of educational training to China – then reflections might be more straightforward. Or Shanghai standards could be compared with Greece, which has a similar rote learning ethos and regulatory state control in education. But for the vast surface of the globe, Chinese education is completely alien. Knowing that Shanghainese 15-year-olds are very good at reading doesn't mean that they actually understand, enjoy or critically engage. After all, in China, cram schools train students to memorize several essays which can then be regurgitated to suit a variety of standardized exam questions. English comprehension is learned from a practiced analysis of sentence construction. This is not to say that everyone does it, or that there aren't brilliant students in China, but it is worth pointing out some trends.

The reality is that Chinese educational, social, parental and peer pressure combine to lock students into reciting the curriculum. Pass and you succeed; fail and you lose (and in English, for example, there are clear pass and fail answers with no grey area in between). Even though the West believes that students need to revise only what they need to revise to pass, a recent study shows that 'whereas the Western expectation may be that tutorials are an opportunity for student discussion of lecture material, by contrast [Chinese] learners are aware of the fact that class time is short and so they would prefer to discuss issues with their class-mates during their own informal "tutorials" after the official one' (Gutierrez and Dyson 2009: 376). As a result, they don't ask questions because they would be a distraction. Passing is the goal. I have given up asking students why they have chosen their specific majors because almost none of them have. It is the parents that decide what they will study in university (although admittedly this parental authority is relaxing somewhat amongst some urban middle classes). Students spend seven years of their lives studying for the Gaokao (the dreaded A Level equivalent) with the simple goal of going to a good university, leading to a good (i.e., financially secure) job. Little else matters. A recent *New York Times* vignette described the role of the cram school or 'memorization factory' that starts at 6:30 every morning and goes until 10 p.m. every day: The 'all-male corps of head teachers doles out lessons', it says, 'and frequently punishments, with military rigor; their job security and bonuses depend on raising their students' test scores' (Larmer 2014).

Chinese teachers are the masters of teaching to the test. This is not much different from the contemporary instrumentalism within the Western model of education, but often – unlike the West – Chinese teachers push their students to get the highest grades. China, as we know, celebrates the STEM subjects, and in one Chinese university Western exchange students recently complained that they could not keep up with the level of maths that was being taught, a classic case of the gap in standards between the UK and China that ex-Secretary of State for Education Michael Gove regularly alluded to, you might think. Here was a clear evidence of maths standards being far superior in China to the UK. Actually, no; the reality was more mundane. The engineering lecturer in question admitted that the maths was unnecessarily hard, but he wanted to win a national maths prizes – using his students – in order to improve his career chances. So, in reality, all students were being taught the wrong level of maths – an *inappropriate* level of maths – for entirely self-aggrandizing and instrumental reasons. In China, this is not atypical, with students seen as a servant of the lecturer.

The *New York Times* report stated that teachers at pre-Gaokao cram schools have to teach huge classes for up to 17 hours a day.

> Teachers whose classes finish in last place at year's end can expect to be fired. It's no wonder that teachers' motivational methods can be tough. Besides rapping knuckles with rulers … some teachers pit them against one another in practice-test 'death matches' – the losers must remain standing all morning. In one much-discussed case, the mother of a tardy student was forced to stand outside her son's class for a week as punishment.
>
> *(Larmer 2014)*

Competition

China is unique in its historic development. A society that, in just 100 years, has suffered the various vicissitudes of imperial rule, internecine violence, wartime destruction, Communist revolution, a brutal Cultural Revolution, societal regimentation and capitalist expansion has resulted in a strangely individuated society. Its communitarian pretensions are still very much in evidence on the surface, but actually, individual survivalism is regularly a pragmatic response to these ideological mood swings.

The ever-present pressure to succeed – to pass exams – finds expression in ugly competition with one's school friends. In a rare academic report surveying attitudes to achievement in China (admittedly taken ten years ago), one unnamed lecturer described the attitude of school children in class: 'you see around you students who are better than you and this generates competition, as all want to be better than each other' (Simon 2000: 117). The battle for places means that very little quarter is given to fellow classmates as their success may result in you missing out on that prized university place or employment position – a worry that now affects all students of all social classes as unemployment rates amongst graduates rises.

Cheating is a fine art, almost a rite of passage. Arthur Lu, an engineering student who graduated from Beijing's Tsinghua University, observed that 'it's not that students can't do the work. They just see it as a way of saving time' (Jacobs 2010). Indeed, cheating is simply a reality given that the exam is such a crucial decider in who gets on and who stays behind. In one school in Hubei Province in 2013, teachers frisked students to ensure that they were not bringing any crib notes in to the exam hall, finding mobile phones hidden in their underwear and radio trans- mitters camouflaged as erasers. These actions triggered a riot as parents smashed windows and damaged staff cars while demanding their children's right to cheat. One parent said: 'We want fairness. There is no fairness if you do not let us cheat' (Yang 2013). After all, when everyone cheats, attempting to stop cheating seems unfair.

The apparent contradiction between individual competition and collectivist sloganeering (a capitalist state with socialist pretensions) can be explained in historic terms. For Chinese philosophers since ancient times there has tended to be no such thing as freedom of will. Instead, the cultivation of the individual only finds meaning within a complex web of social, political, and otherworldly forces. The individual, from the time of Confucius and Mencius, has been a subsumed: a sub- ordinate, 'responsible citizen'. This training in controlled moral agency continues to this day, ironically, in an atheistic, nationalistic guise. One way to understand the social ethos of familial piety is to recall the working class attitude that suffused Britain until the much-hyped 'end of deference'. The working class may not have believed it, indeed many criticized it, but it still infused the individual with a creeping sense of stratified social stigma. We knew our place, and even if parents wanted their children to have the educational opportunities that they themselves had been denied, it was sometimes difficult for some to believe that they should aspire to social elevation above their station. A generation ago, it was common to be told, by parents and career advisers alike, that Oxford and Cambridge was for 'them', not for people like 'us'. Similar voluntary submission to social convention, whether one believes in it or not, is a commonplace in China.

One Chinese graduate expressed her frustration:

> We all have to study Chinese, Mathematics, English and Physics to take the National University Entrance Examination, in order to go to university, no matter if we want to study music, or chemistry, or we are more interested in drawing. Anyone who does poorly in their academic performance will be marked down as a 'bad' student. Such a label will bring the student orchestrated humiliation from their teachers, parents, friends and classmates.
>
> *(Huang Chongyao quoted in Williams 2013a)*

Cute images of junior schoolchildren wearing red Communist Party Young Pioneer neckerchiefs don't really symbolize the pervasive reach of the Party; rather, the neckerchief is an eye-catching way of marking out the good students. It is not uncommon for students who don't perform to be denied neckerchiefs by the teacher in order to mark them out – a modern-day black spot – reinforced by the exclusionary behaviour towards those students by their classmates under direct or implied instruction of the authorities and parents. It is a simple stockade mentality to humiliate errant behaviour into submission.

While Western students might report such ignominy as an act of bullying, many Chinese students are still prepared to recognize it as their duty to roll with the punches – literally sometimes. Somewhere in between these two poles (Western complaint and Asian docility) might be useful.

Between the Western aversion to pressure and the Confucian piety of Chinese youth lies the recognition that education is difficult, stressful and often intellectually confrontational but not burdensome, incessant and soul-destroying. Surely, in the West and East, common sense needs to prevail. Good education challenges the student – and this is the nature of its transformative potential. At least Chinese students hold on to this truth, however much their transformation is ultimately deemed to be pragmatically material rather than metaphysical. But after the brute reality of the late 20th century experienced by many living Chinese, maybe it is excusable – or at least understandable – that they are prepared to put up with a little more in order to succeed to an easy life.

Just as the Chinese state has had to develop rigid social structures to cope with autarkic tendencies over the years, so the people themselves have developed attitudes of mind to deal with autarky. Even though education is clearly viewed as a means to self-improvement, it is also confused with the need for self-preservation. One student notes, 'Studying is the only way to get out of my hometown' (*Economist* 2012). Competition is rife, and students who get better marks than others are respected but also envied. When 10 million students are competing for 6.5 million university places, friendships are a luxury. It is these socially embedded norms that corrode the notion of a collegiate educational project. Even when there are no grade quotas, students are fiercely competitive, criticizing their marks compared to other students. Ultimately, the possibility to enter a Master's programme is reliant on your grades, so someone getting higher marks is a potential threat. One Chinese lecturer's harsh assessment put it this way: 'Independence of thought is subordinated to the demands of rote learning. The students who emerge from this system often find it difficult to make basic social engagement, let alone intellectual collaboration' (*Economist* 2012).

Even though this competitive tension is seldom overtly expressed (Chinese universities are certainly not hotbeds of revolt),[2] these underlying (latent) social tensions infuse the way that students view their education. China is keen to manage the growing parental resentment at the pressures to get into a good Chinese university and the shrinking gains derived from from being there. As a result, in a pilot study in Shanghai Municipality and Zhejiang from 2015, students will be evaluated on their personal and social qualities as well as their academic records, requiring 'secondary school students to present a record of information relating to moral standards, physical health, general culture, such as hobbies, and social or community engagement and contribution, such as volunteering' (Morgan and Wu 2015). This will do nothing to alleviate the tense inequalities within Chinese educational practices. As one research paper shows, disadvantages affect children in rural areas but specifically those children of poorly educated fathers who do not have the economic or social status to know anyone in the 'it's-who-you-know' process (Hannum, An and Hua-Yu 2011). But more fundamentally, Professor Andrew Kipnis points out that across all social classes, 'exactly what type of education will enhance the quality of the people is still open to debate' (Kipnis 2011: 66).

Pragmatism

For a long time, modern China has been a society governed by the primary goal of social stability. 'Pragmatism' has been a label that has been applied to China across history, and officially sanctioned in the late '70s, but today's politicized pragmatism of studied disinterest is palpable, combining an ethereal Chinese demand for 'harmony' with a Western need for evidence-based justification. The Chinese experience is described by one award-winning author, Tao Zhu, as 'anti-theoretical pragmatism "with Chinese characteristics"' (Zhu 2009: 92).

The much-cited phrase of Deng Xiaoping, that China should 'cross the river by feeling the stones' exemplifies the idea that you should take the path that provides the best, safest route to success. Chinese state operatives – including, of course, the education sector management hierarchy – endorse what works and ditch what doesn't pay off without batting an eyelid. As such the education that is lauded is that which provides a recipe for financial opportunities and stability. Education, education, education in China is merely defined by results, results, results and political continuity.

Sadly, even in explorative, risk-taking China, survivalism seems to be the over-arching social policy framework. Lawrence Lau, professor of Economic Development at Stanford University, says, 'Chinese economic reformers are characterized by their pragmatism – they are willing to try almost anything – whatever works – but they will just as readily abandon whatever that proves not to work' (Lau 2008: 2). For many ordinary people, their day-to-day experience is one of protecting what they have, but even businesses, education and government agencies are affected by such a cautious approach.

Undoubtedly, risk-taking is laudable in an age of precaution, but the ability to ditch ideas also suggests that there is very little belief in the object under con-sideration. After a spate of ludicrous, high-profile architectural vanity projects, Premier Xi Jinping condemned 'weird architecture' and instead called for more representative, sedate and traditional projects. As a result, university architecture departments had funding – or more importantly 'political will' – cut, immediately. Many innocent researchers of exploratory design were left high and dry as uni-versities ditched their programmes overnight for something more conventional. Worse still, President Xi Jinping's crackdown on graft and corruption in order to consolidate his political control has meant that internet access is regularly curtailed, with virtual provider networks that circumvent the Chinese firewall being blocked and rendered ineffective. The result is that while China puffs itself out as a significant player in global education, internally professors and students are lucky if they can access Google Scholar once a week. China may say that it wants more academic freedom (and it was only in 2010 when Chinese Premier Wen Jiaobao launched his education reform that insisted that schools and universities prioritize 'critical thinking'), but by December 2014 the new Premier Xi Jinping was unashamedly calling for significant controls on the higher education sector in order to create 'socialist universities with Chinese characteristics' (Hunwick 2014).

Many commentators in the West see this illiberal shift as renewed evidence of the iron hand of communism. But that couldn't be further from the truth. China is not going back to communism, but it is simply wary of what capitalism will bring. It is symptomatic of China's inability to reconcile its own contradictions. It is simply ham fisted pragmatic politics with serious and dangerous consequences.

Fudan University kowtows to the new paranoia by stating that it will 'strengthen educational guidance' for its young teachers so they might 'grasp Marx's way of reaching his viewpoint' (AFP 2014). In December 2013 Shanghai professor of law Zhang Xuezhong was sacked for advocating free speech and the rule of law. Obviously, this is a retreat from free expression and from academic openness. But ironically, whereas there is a general perception that China is culturally wedded to ideological clampdowns, much of it is ideology-lite managerialism. Communism as a social glue has disappeared from Chinese society, religion doesn't have much of a foothold, and so, the direction of society is guided by tenuous Confucian morality and a bureaucratic group-think. On this flimsy basis, lived practical experience is the ultimate test of what is correct. In essence, China preaches functional utility.

The irony is that China is learning from the West, while the West thinks it is discovering the real China. No wonder, then, that UK education policy wonks are also keen to embrace similar educational shortcuts to economic growth. No wonder, too, that John Dewey – a pragmatic philosopher who was heavily influenced by Chinese society in the 1920s – is now high on the readings of Chinese education officials (a translation of Dewey's works is currently being carried out at East China Normal University in Shanghai). Dewey spent two years in China, arriving immediately after the pro-democracy May 4th protests in 1919, and heavily influenced that pro-Western movement. His ideas were then developed, amended and interpreted to suit the changing conditions of 1920s China. In 1941, British philosopher Alfred North Whitehead stated, 'If you want to understand Confucius, read John Dewey. And if you want to understand Dewey, read Confucius' (Zhang 2013: 66). No wonder that many Western and Chinese educators are rediscovering that troublesome ideas are not worth bothering with if there are no immediate tangible beneficial consequences. Conflicting ideas, the stuff of education, muddy the waters of an easy life and social quiescence, it seems.

The pragmatic approach of Chinese education presents, I would suggest, a significant danger that is being ignored due to the Western intoxication with China's educational successes. Now that so many Western policymakers are becoming uncritical supporters of China, it is necessary to move the debate on. This is not necessarily to criticize China but rather to turn the spotlight back on ourselves.

When Sidney and Beatrice Webb grew increasingly demoralised by the moral and economic collapse in the West in the 1930s they saw immediate salvation in the Stalinist Soviet system, which they dubbed 'a new civilization' (Webb and Webb 1936). In the same way, many in the West are losing their critical faculties, either blinded by suitably impressive (although often dubious) performance data from China or because they *want* to be swept along by the dynamism of others.

It is ironic that in a debate about the Academy, where it is all about judgment and open enquiry, that so many are willing to accede to unsubstantiated reports of China's rise. But it is easy to see how the impressive achievements of education in China – its social status, the respect for professors, the youthful acceptance of hard-work, the desire to succeed, everything that seems to have ebbed out of the British system – means that British teachers and politicians would like to wish it into existence.

But it would be much more important to assess why the British education system is in such a parlous state than to pretend that we can get a turnkey Chinese solution to Western problems. I hope that this essay has been a useful start to the debate. I welcome comments and questions.

Notes

1   National Bureau of Statistics of China, 2014, Number of students of formal education by type and level (2013). The figure cited is the higher education enrolment data and includes 6.25 million undergraduates in Adult Higher Education Institutions, 12 million attending 'Short-cycle Courses' and 18 million postgraduates.
2   '[S]tudents suffer from intense insecurity, self-doubt and anxiety about their future lives. Inevitably, these pressures lead many Chinese students to choose to detach themselves from China's critical intelligentsia and instead align themselves with a much more politically apathetic and compliant professional working class' (Xiaojun Yan, quoted in Goodman 2014).

References

AFP (2014) China universities vow ideology clampdown on staff, students, Yahoo News, 1 September: http://news.yahoo.com/china-universities-vow-ideology-clampdown-staff-students-132939456.html (accessed 17 July 2016).

Altbach, P. G., Androushchak, G., Kuzminov, Y., Yudkevich, M. and Reisberg, L. (2013) *The Global Future of Higher Education and the Academic Profession: The BRICs and the United States*, London: Palgrave Macmillan.

Buchanan, P. (2012) The big rethink part 9: rethinking architectural education, *The Architectural Review*, 28 September: http://www.architectural-review.com/archive/campaigns/the-big-rethink/the-big-rethink-part-9-rethinking-architectural-education/8636035.article (accessed 10 June 2016).

Cameron, D. (2012) My visit can begin a relationship to benefit China, Britain and the world, *Guardian*, 2 December: https://www.theguardian.com/commentisfree/2013/dec/02/david-cameron-my-visit-to-china (accessed 10 June 2016).

Chang, L. T. (2009) *Factory Girls: From Village to City in a Changing China*, New York: Spiegel and Grau.

Economist (2012) Testing times, Analects: China, *Economist*, 13 June: http://www.economist.com/blogs/analects/2012/06/university-entrance-exams (accessed 1 August 2016).

Furedi, F. (2013) Pisa: top of the class for dumbing down, spiked, 3 December: http://www.spiked-online.com/newsite/article/pisa_top_of_the_class_for_dumbing_down/14375#.V7w6Mvl97X4 (accessed 11 July 2016).

Goodman, D. S. G. (2014) China's universities and social change: expectations, aspirations, and consequences, paper presented at the China in the Global Academic Landscapes Conference, Herrenhausen Castle, Hanover, 11–12 December 2014.

Griffiths, M. B. and Jesper, Z. (2014) Bittersweet China: new discourses of hardship and social organisation, *Journal of Current Chinese Affairs*, 43(4): 143–174.

Gutierrez, F. and Dyson, L. E. (2009) Confucian or fusion?: perceptions of Confucian-heritage students with respect to their university studies in Australia, *The International Journal of Learning*, 16(5): 373–384.

Hammond, P. (2007) *Media, War and Postmodernity*, London and New York: Routledge.

Han, T. (2014) The Chinese student code, *The World of Chinese*, 5 April: http://www.theworldofchinese.com/2014/08/love the nation-the-chinese-student-code/ (accessed 1 August 2016).

Hannum, E., An, X. and Hua-Yu, S. C. (2011) Examinations and educational opportunity in China: mobility and bottlenecks for the rural poor, *Oxford Review of Education*, 37(2): 267 305.

Hunwick, R. F. (2014) Xi Jinping calls for ideological control on Chinese universities, *Telegraph*, 30 December: http://www.telegraph.co.uk/news/worldnews/asia/china/11317579/Xi-Jinping-calls-for-ideological-control-on-Chinese-universities.html (accessed 1 August 2016).

Jacobs, A. (2010) Rampant fraud threat to China's brisk ascent, *The New York Times*, 6 October: http://www.nytimes.com/2010/10/07/world/asia/07fraud.html?pagewanted=all&_r=0 (accessed 17 July 2016).

Joshi, D. (2010) The Chinese are a pragmatic lot: Tom Doctoroff, JWT China, My JWT, https://my.jwt.com/public/jwt_net.nsf/91d6fa0385b640a386256fc4001f1a53/186a95e13b90c2918525770a004922a7 (accessed 17 July 2016).

Kipnis, A. B. (2011) *Governing Educational Desire: Culture, Politics and Schooling in China*, Chicago: University of Chicago Press.

Kirkebæk, M. J., Du, X-Y. and Jensen, A. A. (2013) *Teaching and Learning Culture: Negotiating the Context*, Rotterdam: Sense Publishers.

Larmer, B. (2014) Inside a Chinese test-prep factory, *The New York Times*, 31 December: http://www.nytimes.com/2015/01/04/magazine/inside-a-chinese-test-prep-factory.html?_r=0 (accessed 17 July 2016).

Lau, L. J. (2008) Thirty years of Chinese economic reform: reasons for its success and future directions, *Internet and Network Economics, Lecture Notes in Computer Science*, 5385: 2–3.

Marcus, J. (2013) Fraud fears rocket as Chinese seek a place at any price, *Times Higher Education*, 13 June: https://www.timeshighereducation.com/news/fraud-fears-rocket-as-chinese-seek-a-place-at-any-price/2004704.article (accessed 17 July 2016).

Morgan, W. J. and Wu, B. (2015) Why reforms to China's college entrance exam are so revolutionary, *The Conversation UK*, 16 January: https://theconversation.com/why-reforms-to-chinas-college-entrance-exam-are-so-revolutionary-36048(accessed 10 July 2016).

National Bureau of Statistics of China (2014) Number of students of formal education by type and level (2013), *China Statistical Yearbook 2014*, Beijing: China Statistics Press: http://www.stats.gov.cn/tjsj/ndsj/2014/indexeh.htm (accessed 14 March 2016).

Ng, S. S. N. (2010) Mathematics teaching in Hong Kong pre-schools: mirroring the Chinese cultural aspiration towards learning? Hong Kong: The Hong Kong Institute of Education: http://www.cimt.org.uk/journal/ng.pdf (accessed 16 August 2016).

Ng, S. S. N. (2014) Mathematics teaching in Hong Kong pre-schools: mirroring the Chinese cultural aspiration towards learning? *International Journal for Mathematics Teaching and Learning*, 15(1): 1–36.

Simon, L. (2000) Examination orientation and the opportunity structure in Chinese education: case studies of Kunming High School, a thesis submitted for the degree of Doctor of Philosophy in the Contemporary China Centre Research School of Pacific and Asian Studies, The Australian National University, November 2000.

Webb, S. and Webb, B. (1936) *Is Soviet Communism a New Civilization?*, London: The Left Review.

Williams, A. (2013a) Such stuff as Chinese dreams are made on, *Times Higher Education*, 27 June: https://www.timeshighereducation.com/features/culture/such-stuff-as-chinese-dreams-are-made-on/2005019.article (accessed 17 July 2016).

Williams, A. (2013b) Off Piste – drawing inspiration, *Times Higher Education*, 22 August: https://www.timeshighereducation.com/features/off-piste-drawing-inspiration/2006575.article (accessed 18 July 2016).

Xinyuan, Z. (2014) A costly education, *Global Times*, 21 December: http://www.globaltimes.cn/content/897938.shtml (accessed 10 July 2016).

Xueqin, J. (2011) How China kills creativity, *The Diplomat*, 2 July: http://thediplomat.com/2011/07/how-china-kills-creativity/ (accessed 17 August 2016).

Yang, K. (2013) Expel all exam cheats, *South China Morning Post*, 26 June: http://www.scmp.com/comment/insight-opinion/article/1268784/expel-all-exam-cheats (accessed 1 August 2016).

Zhang, H. (2013) *John Dewey, Liang Shuming, and China's Education Reform: Cultivating Individuality*, Lanham, MA: Lexington Books.

Zhu, T. (2009) Cross the river by touching the stones: Chinese architecture and political economy in the reform era 1978–2008, *Architectural Design*, 79(1): 88–93.

INDEX

Page numbers in italics refer to figures. Page numbers in bold refer to tables.

Oakeshott, Michael 101
Obama, Barack 30, 35
Oberlin College 78
occupational licensing 77, 80
offence, in universities 53
Office for Budget Responsibility (UK) 33
Office for Students 95, 98
official government facts 73–5
official government values 72–3
Ofqual 89, 90
Oklahoma Wesleyan University 76
online universities 44
open inquiry: defenses of 69–70; and
    ideology 70–2; proposals to promote
    78–80; and state 72–5
Oxford University 48, 62, 105

Palfreyman, David 103
parental choice 26
parental pressure, in China 121
Parris, Matthew 107
pension schemes, reform of 24
performance culture 8
personal, social and health education
    (PSHE) classes 12
personal literacy 12
petting zoos 105
Pieper, Josef 63
Plato 47, 50; and nature 49
Polanyi, Michael 69
policing: internal policing of faculty
    members 78; of lawyers 77; and medicine
    77
political currency, US dollar as 22
political elites 21
political science 75
post-compulsory education 19, 26, 35, 86
posts, student-experience related 95, 98
pragmatism 125–7
predictability 7, 44
pre-university education 85
private capital 24
Private Industry Councils (PICS), US 25
privatisation 20, 26, 33, 34; of education
    services 27–8, 36–7; of funding 78–9; in
    training and vocational education 29
Privy Council 36
productive dynamism 22, 23, 37n1
professional associations, and free speech
    77, 80
professional fitness 78
Programme for International Student
    Assessment (PISA) 120–1
prosumer 46
prosumption 43

Protestant Ethic and the Spirit of Capitalism
    (Weber) 5
public expenditure, and containment 22–3
Public Private Finance (PFI) initiatives 27,
    37n6
puppy rooms 105
puritans 70

Quacquarelli Symonds (QS) World
    University Rankings 7
quantitative easing 24
quick refutation of relativism 100

radical humanism 48–9
rampant capitalism 21
Raskin, Sarah Bloom 30
Rauch, Jonathan 69
reading skills 121
rebranding 2
reductionism 37n4
Reformation 48
Regent's University London 36
relativism, and student experience 99–100
relevant knowledge 96
Renaissance 48
*Report of the National Committee of Inquiry into
    Higher Education* (Dearing) 93, 94
Republic of Science 69, 78
Research Assessment Exercise (RAE) 7
Research Excellence Framework (REF) 3,
    7, 44, 62
Resource Development International *see*
    Arden University
revelation, Christian 61, 62
Richardson, Louise 112
risk assessments 8
Ritzer, George 1, 4–6, 11, 16; being 43;
    biography of 42–3; interview with Hayes
    42–6; pessimism of 13, 42, 44, 45
RMIT University (Melbourne), graduate
    attributes of 12
Roksa, Josipa 13
rote learning 121, 124

sacred spaces 51, 52
safe spaces 11, 44–5, 55, 62, 106–7, 110
Saint Augustine 70
St. Benedict 64
savings 24
Schleiermacher, Friedrich 49
Scholars at Risk 68
scholarships 27
school voucher schemes 26, 267
Scruton, Roger 60
secondary schools 57

.